How to Choose a
Financial
Advisor

Graydon G. Watters

Additional praise for
How to Choose a Financial Advisor

"An important decision! A qualified teacher through experience and insight. Congratulations!"

— Karen Fisher
   Director, Managed Asset Group
   ScotiaMcLeod Inc.

"A must read for those who need the nuts and bolts to make that critical decision on how to choose a financial quarter-back."

— Stuart McKay
   President
   McKay Financial Management

"Once again Graydon has taken the complex and made it accessible to all. Well done!"

— Jim Lyons
   Manager, Compensation and Benefits
   York University

"Graydon, having you as a guest on Canada's Smart Money Show has really demonstrated both your breadth of experience, and your real desire to deliver understandable, useful advice. Congratulations!"

— Paul Bates
   President & CEO
   Porthmeor Securities Inc.

"Graydon's broad industry experience enables him to offer clear, comprehensive advice valuable to anyone concerned with their financial well-being. I strongly recommend his holistic lifestyle approach to all my clients. My sincere congratulations on another solid effort."

— **Michael Dunn**
    C.F.P., Branch Manager
    DeThomas Financial

"The financial planner who helps you attain your life goals will be your subject matter expert, confidante, and trusted advisor — that makes it most important to choose the right person, and this book tells you how."

— **Carole Griffin**
    Manager, Benefits
    Computing Devices Canada Ltd.

The author wishes to express thanks and appreciation to
Dr. Chuck Chakrapani, Editor, *Money Digest,* Investors Association
of Canada who granted permission to use their material.

Printed and bound in Toronto, Canada.

Copy Editor: Geraldine Kikuta

Design: Bold Graphic Communication Ltd.

Canadian Cataloguing in Publication Data

Watters, Graydon G., 1943–
     How to choose a financial advisor
     ISBN 0-9681285-1-3
     1. Financial planners. 2. Investment advisors.
I. Kikuta, Geraldine. II. Financial Knowledge Inc.
III. Title
HG179.5.W37 1997   332.024   C97-931989-7

Acknowledgements

Today, managing money is a full-time job. It is no longer a luxury for a privileged few. In fact financial planning has become virtually indispensable for those who are serious about their future.

This book is dedicated to the thousands of students and participants who have attended our financial education programs during the last several years. It became very clear through our interactive workshops how desperate the need was for most participants to find that special relationship with a financial professional who could assist them in reaching for and accomplishing their dreams. Individuals, just like you, shared over 200 different traits and characteristics that they would like this special person to have.

I am especially grateful to Andy Billesdon, FKI's own Vice President of Marketing and Sales. His continuous input and creative collaboration of the contents, flow, quotations, and re-working of the manuscript were invaluable. As well, Andy's multiple skills sets, including marketing, sales, training, facilitating, and his wonderful sense of humour, make working with him a pleasurable experience.

Special thanks also to Penny Butt, my administration assistant who wears more hats than I have fingers and toes to count with. I don't know where she finds the extra time to input, re-work, and review all of my writing.

My recognition and thanks go to numerous financial professionals who have supported our company by providing public seminars and client appreciation events throughout the years.

And finally, this book is for Josephine Casey, one of my best friends and life partner who always believes. Her spiritual insights and holistic approach to life are a constant reminder of the balanced lifestyle I desire. Jo, you are the catalyst for much of my personal growth and I sincerely thank you for your strength and support.

About the Author

Graydon G. Watters, B. Comm., F.C.S.I., C.F.P., is the Founder and President of Financial Knowledge Inc. He has devoted thirty-five years to the financial services industry, including a decade in banking and two decades in investment counselling, and several years as an educator. During this time he has assisted thousands of individuals with their investment decisions.

During the last several years Graydon Watters has pioneered the development of several exciting audio-visual presentations on financial and pre-retirement planning education. He wrote the best-selling book, *Financial Pursuit* in 1988 for all age groups; developed a pre-retirement planning course, *Lifestyle Pursuit* in 1990 for the 45 plus age group; wrote the best-seller *Financial Survival for the 21st Century* in 1996 for the baby-boom generation; and wrote *How to Choose a Financial Advisor* in 1997 for all Canadians.

Graydon Watters facilitates numerous seminars and workshops every year; has been on radio and television; and has been quoted in many newspapers and financial publications. Testimonials to Graydon refer to his enthusiasm, commitment, dynamism, and innovative educational programs and systems. His seminars and workshops are tailored to suit the specific audience and he has lectured corporate, professional, and public audiences throughout North America.

Financial Knowledge Inc. is Canada's number one corporate generic educational company. FKI designs and delivers educational materials, publications, seminars, and workshops for employers and their employees, professional associations, and public audiences. The main emphasis of their presentations is achieving financial security, a balanced lifestyle, and a retirement with dignity.

Graydon Watters and his associate facilitators are available for seminars, workshops, and keynote addresses. Please contact the following:

Financial Knowledge Inc.
279 Yorkland Blvd., North York, Ontario M2J 1S7
Tel. (416) 499-5466 Fax (416) 499-7748

Table of Contents

*To Josephine and our children
Andrew, Christina, Megan, Carolyn,
J-P, and Matthew for their ongoing
love and support.*

Preface

The road to retirement for most Canadians will be much tougher to negotiate than many envision. Government debt is still a major problem — $800 billion combined federal and provincial debt and another $600 billion unfunded liability for the Canada Pension Plan (CPP). Of the 18 million working Canadians, 8 million do not have an employer pension plan or an RRSP. The large middle-class group of Canadians is rapidly shrinking to either end of the spectrum creating two groups, poles apart — the haves versus the have-nots — and it is not a pretty picture.

"By the street of by-and-by, one arrives at the house of never."
— Cervantes

When we ask participants in our seminars, "At what age do you plan to retire?" most respond, "Mid to late 50s." When we ask, "What degree of financial planning are you doing to ensure your early retirement?" many respond, "Very little" or "Nothing at all!" Many other surveys show most Canadians are not pension planned. What does it take to get the message across to the large number of people who are doing no planning at all?

Perhaps the major reason Canadians procrastinate about financial planning is they don't know how to get started. We spend more time in our seminars on the subject of how to choose a financial planner/advisor than any other area. People will often offer me a cheque for their life savings after experiencing our program saying, "I trust you Graydon, you've got all the characteristics and traits I'm looking for." Of course if I could take their cheques their employer wouldn't have sponsored our company in the first place. There would be a conflict of interest between offering pure generic education and one-on-one financial planning and/or product sales and implementation.

It is our belief at **Financial Knowledge Inc. (FKI)**, the company I founded in 1984, that you can't mix education and product implementation. Major corporate clients helped me make my choice to retire as a stockbroker to pursue a new career as an educator because they would not provide education for employees if there were products sold. In my 23 plus years as a stockbroker, I learned that those clients with the most knowledge were the ones who were the most successful and with whom I enjoyed the best relationships. They would stay through the worst bear markets knowing assuredly that a new bull market was inevitable. Why? Because it has always been that way: bulls follow bears, follow bulls, follow bears — that is the rhythm of the cycles in the markets.

Whether you are a seasoned investor looking to evaluate your current relationship or a novice investor looking to get started, this book will provide the tools you need to find that special person who can help you with your financial planning. Beyond your primary relationship with a spouse or partner, this relationship ranks right near the top. After all, we're dealing with your second most important asset — your financial health which ranks right behind your most important asset — your physical health.

Part I

PLANNING IS THE PROCESS TO EMPOWERMENT

One

The Dawning of a New Age

As we bear down on the 21st Century, the challenges facing us with regard to our financial management or mismanagement are many. Ask yourself, "Will my current asset allocation and investment strategies provide the purchasing power I'll need for a retirement that could last 20, 30, or even 40 years or more?"

The world we share is changing so rapidly it is difficult for many to cope. New knowledge is evolving at breakneck speed driven by computers and the technological revolution. Change is rampant! It will not be the strongest or the smartest of human beings who will survive — it will be those of us who are most adaptable to **CHANGE!**

"As a field, however fertile cannot be fruitful without cultivation, neither can a mind without learning."
— Cicero

Yesterday is gone. Tomorrow is a result of
what we think and do today.

If you fail to learn, grow, or develop at the speed of change or faster, then change will be a threat to you. What can you do to tackle change? Adapt the following habits of self-improvement to tackle change head-on:

- Learn something new every day.
- Prioritize personal self-development time.
- Schedule a time percentage each day for learning.
- Become a dedicated lifelong learner.

"There is a bulldozer of change sweeping the planet. If you are not part of the bulldozer you will become part of the road."
— Frank Ogden

The financial services world is also changing rapidly. The print and electronic media have coverage every day on topics such as

- salaries, commissions, wrap fees, and segregated accounts
- incentive-based performance fees, and trailers
- competition from foreign markets/global diversification
- deep discounters, no frills
- front-load, back-load, low-load, and no-load funds
- competition of financial service companies — banks, trusts, investment dealers, and insurance companies

What do you make of all this news? How do you deal with this much change? What asset allocation and investment strategies are appropriate for you? What mixture of cash reserves, stocks, bonds, or mutual funds is right for you? And which mutual funds would you choose out of over 1,400 available?

Obviously, you need to have an edge, and the edge is education. You owe it to yourself to learn as much as you can about financial planning. You can also engage the services of a financial professional to help guide you through the maze.

What Do People Really Want?

In simplistic terms most people simply want to know how to establish a financial plan with a person they can trust, and they need to know what action steps to take to begin the process. Sounds easy, eh! If it were, everybody would already have a professional advisor and be well along the way to financial security.

The number one reason people invest is for retirement. Investors are taking more responsibility today due to the uncertainty of government programs and employment due to corporate re-engineering, downsizing, and early leave options.

Once the investor has made the decision to invest, the next most important questions are "how to and who with?"

Most investors are overwhelmed by the investment choices available. They have neither the time nor the experience, and they lack the information to make timing decisions to buy, sell, or hold crucial investments. They need guidance to develop an asset allocation strategy to reach their retirement goals. And they expect their financial professionals to educate them.

Financial Planner or Advisor?

Thousands of Canadians have attended our employer-sponsored seminars during the last several years and the one issue that has become abundantly clear is that very few people really know the role of a financial planner.

Most people confuse investment planning or specific investment security selection with the profession of financial planning. The true financial planner is qualified to provide advice on every aspect of your financial and lifestyle goals and objectives (see Chart 1–1).

TRADITIONAL BUSINESS APPROACH   Chart 1–1

FINANCIAL PLANNER
Financial Plans, Goals and Objectives,
Will, Estate, and Tax Planning,
Asset Allocation and Investment Strategy

BANK OR TRUST AGENT
Loans, Savings, Chequing,
Mortgages, Estates, GICs, Term Deposits

INSURANCE AGENT
Life, Term, Disability
and General Insurance

INVESTMENT COUNSELLOR
Descretionary Portfolio Management
Asset Allocation

MUTUAL FUND AGENT
Mutual Funds, GICs,
Balanced Growth Plans

STOCKBROKER
Stocks, Bonds, CSBs, RRSPs
CTBs, Tax Shelters

ACCOUNTANT
Tax and Estate Planning,
Accounting, Bookkeeping

DIRECT PURCHASE
No–Load,
Mutual Funds, GICs

DISCOUNT BROKERS
Stocks, Bonds,
Mutual Funds, RRSPs

THE CO-OPERATIVE MANAGEMENT APPROACH   Chart 1–2

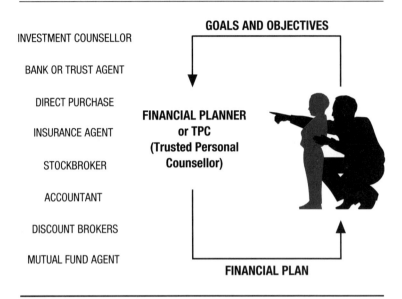

GOALS AND OBJECTIVES

INVESTMENT COUNSELLOR

BANK OR TRUST AGENT

DIRECT PURCHASE

FINANCIAL PLANNER or TPC (Trusted Personal Counsellor)

INSURANCE AGENT

STOCKBROKER

ACCOUNTANT

DISCOUNT BROKERS

MUTUAL FUND AGENT

FINANCIAL PLAN

A planner is the key person who co-ordinates your financial goals into a coherent plan and then works either alone or with advisors to implement the various elements in your plan. For example, the completion of an estate plan for a high net worth, sophisticated individual may require the financial planner to engage the services of several professionals including a lawyer, accountant (tax specialist), insurance agent, financial advisor, or investment counsellor. Although most Canadians think they need a financial planner, what they really need is a financial advisor who is an investment expert and a strong financial-planning generalist.

How did the financial-planning intermediary terminology become this complicated? Thank the media for the most part. Pick up any printed material or tune into the electronic media and the most common term generally used to describe anyone and everyone in the industry is **financial planner**.

Prior to deregulation in the mid-1980s there were four pillars of finance in Canada — banks, trusts, investment dealers, and insurance companies. Today, it's hard to tell which businesses these institutions are in as they continue to merge, network, takeover, buy-out, or form strategic alliances with each other. It is from these crossing disciplines that the financial planner emerged.

Financial Planning Survey

When we ask Canadians what they think of financial professionals, many have very little respect for or trust in them. And that is unfortunate because these same people desperately need help with their financial plans.

Before we can even start to explore who may be attracted to a career in financial planning, we should ask the question, "What's in a name?"

Most people use the term "financial planner" to describe anyone employed in the financial services industry. This is unfair and hardly provides justice for the person who truly is qualified. A financial planner usually carries the designation Certified Financial Planner (CFP) or Registered Financial Planner (RFP) both of which require six substantial courses and a minimum of two years' practical experience as well as 30 hours per year of continuing education credits. The RFP designation in addition requires an annual written exam and financial plan to maintain a licence.

It's an absolute minefield for the typical investor to sort out who's who in the financial services industry when stockbrokers, insurance agents, mutual fund specialists, and virtually anyone else can use the term financial planner. Most investors don't know what they really need, who they need to work with, and which type of financial professional to select to fulfill their goals and objectives.

We surveyed several hundred participants in our seminars earlier this year and asked several questions, one of which is detailed in Table 1–3.

FKI PARTICIPANT SURVEY			Table 1–3
1. You have decided it is time to review every aspect of your future financial and lifestyle plans. Who would you choose to work with?			
Insurance agent	2%	Do my own plan	13%
Accountant	4%	Mutual fund advisor	13%
Bank or Trust officer	7%	Financial planner	51%
Stockbroker	10%		

FINANCIAL INTERMEDIARIES — MUTUAL FUNDS

Table 1–4

Description	Financial Planners	Mutual Fund Agents	Stockbrokers	Investment Counsellors	Insurance Agents
Offers broad range of financial products	Maybe	Yes	Yes	Yes	Maybe
Value-added advice	Yes	Yes	Yes	Yes	Yes
Active management by agent	Yes	Yes	Yes	Yes	Yes
Investment knowledge level	High	Medium/High	High	High	Medium/High
Agent a mutual fund specialist	Maybe	Yes	Maybe	Maybe	Maybe
Single family or multiple families	Multiple	Multiple	Multiple	Multiple	Single/Multiple
Load or commission	Probably	Probably	Probably	Unlikely	Probably
Front-end	Yes	Yes	Yes	No	Yes
Back-end	Yes	Yes	Yes	No	Yes
No-load	Yes	No	No	No	No
Set-up fee	Maybe	No	No	No	No
Hourly fee	Maybe	No	No	No	No
% of assets	Maybe	No	No	Yes	No

Description	Accountants	Direct Purchase No-Load	Banks and Trusts	Discount Brokers
Offers broad range of financial products	Maybe	No	No	Yes
Value-added advice	Yes	Limited	Limited	No
Active management by agent	Yes	No	No	No
Investment knowledge level	Medium/High	Medium	Low	Low
Agent a mutual fund specialist	Maybe	Limited	No	No
Single family or multiple families	Multiple	Single	Single	Multiple
Load or commission	Probably	Unlikely	Unlikely	Probably
Front-end	Yes	No	No	Yes
Back-end	Yes	No	No	Yes
No-load	Yes	Yes	Yes	No
Set-up fee	Maybe	Yes	No	No
Hourly fee	Maybe	No	No	No
% of assets	Maybe	No	No	No

In response to this question, the overwhelming choice of a financial planner to review every aspect of your financial and lifestyle goals is probably the right choice. However, if I told you that the typical fee-based financial planner charges $125 to $250 per hour and that when your plan is complete you often have to find other financial intermediaries to implement it, such as buying or selling securities, drafting a will, or purchasing an insurance policy, was it really a financial planner you needed? For instance the buying and selling of securities would normally be transacted through a stockbroker, a discount broker, or a mutual fund advisor. Financial planners may or may not be licensed to implement these transactions.

Obviously we need a better understanding of what constitutes financial planning and what the various financial intermediaries offer in terms of services. You will notice that Table 1–4 for financial intermediaries specifies mutual funds. Why? It is my belief that a unit trust or packaged money approach is the best and most efficient way to invest for the vast majority of Canadians, and mutual funds are the most suitable investment for as much as 90% of the population.

Ask yourself, "Do I have the time, knowledge, temperament, and adequate resources to manage my affairs?" Most investors do not! Perhaps this explains the tremendous growth experienced in the mutual fund industry — $4 billion in 1982 to $250 billion in

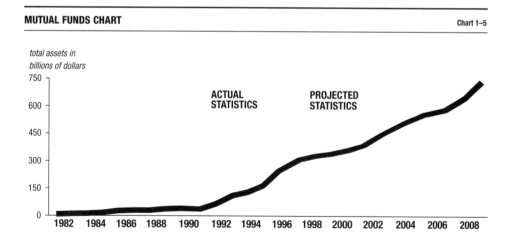

MUTUAL FUNDS CHART Chart 1–5

total assets in billions of dollars

ACTUAL STATISTICS   PROJECTED STATISTICS

mid-1997 — projected to grow to $600 to $700 billion during the next decade. Demographics driven by the boomer generation also explain this phenomenal growth where mutual funds have become the investment of choice for most boomers.

Distribution Channels for Mutual Funds

Typically mutual funds can be purchased through the following four channels:

1. Banks, trust companies, and other deposit-taking institutions
2. Investment dealers, independent brokers, mutual fund specialists, and financial planners
3. Insurance companies
4. Direct sales forces

Wishes versus Goals

Is there a need for financial advice? You betcha! My experience during an investment and banking career that spanned over three decades is that most people have very vague financial wishes rather than concrete goals. Let me ask you a question, "Is a lottery

A big target to hit!

ticket a form of financial planning?" Of course not! Yet for many Canadians who have given up all hope of achieving financial independence, that is their plan. Their mindset is either they're going to win the big prize ($2 million) or they're going to get by on next to nothing by the time they retire.

The purchase of a lottery ticket or any other form of gambling is a wish, not a goal. Witness the conversation you have with yourself when you purchase a lottery ticket. "I wish I could win $2 million — all my dreams would come true!" Obviously this is not a goal. To establish a financial planning goal you would have to visualize, articulate, time-bound, and ideally put in writing what you are trying to achieve. Only then would you have a focused goal.

"An objective without a plan is a dream."
— W. J. Redden

Buying a lottery ticket is much easier then buying a security. When making an investment the first question would be, "Which security should I purchase?" Most investors don't have a clue where to start, nor do they have the time or inclination to proceed on their own. This bodes well for financial advisors. Investors need the services and advice that the professional advisor can provide. So how do you find a financial advisor that meets your unique needs and objectives? Chapter 2 has the answers.

Two

Choose Your Partnerships Carefully

PRIOR TO DEREGULATION OF THE FINANCIAL SERVICE INDUSTRY IN the early 1980s, people entered into a partnership with you for only two reasons:

1. You had a product or service they desired.
2. They trusted you.

After deregulation partnerships were formed for these additional reasons:

1. Price competition/discounting
2. Greater competition/four pillars merged

Most of this century the pillars were in very distinct businesses — banking, trusts, investment dealers, and insurance companies. Today most financial service companies offer multiple services to gain market share from the competition. Twenty-first century partnerships are now being formed for these additional reasons:

1. Quality service
2. Customer satisfaction
3. Superior performance returns
4. Technological capability
5. Ability to provide in-depth education

Prior to deregulation financial planning was an event; after deregulation financial planning became a process; and in the 21st

Century financial planning will require a holistic approach to one's affairs (see Table 2–1).

SIX POWERS OF SUCCESS	Table 2–1
Physical Health	**Personal Fulfillment**
Right Nutrition/Diet	Emotional Health
Regular Exercise	Peace of Mind
Balanced Lifestyle	Spiritual Inquiry
Stress Management	Intellectual Satisfaction
Personal Control	**Precious Relationships**
Philosophy	Changing Roles
Challenges/Opportunities	Family
Positive Mental Attitude	Friends/Social
Choices/Start Today	Coping with Loss
Personal Skills	**Pursuit of Financial Freedom**
Goal Setting	Pay Yourself First
Objectives/Plan of Action	Cash Management
Self-Starter/Motivated	Asset Allocation
Creative	Investment Strategy
Communications	Retirement Planning

Six Powers of Success

In the design of our master program Lifestyle Pursuit, we embrace a holistic approach to wealth management based on the **Six Powers of Success**. So, let me ask you a question. Suppose you had the sixth power, *Pursuit of Financial Freedom*, to the exclusion of or imbalance with the other five powers. What would you have? What did Marilyn Munroe, Elvis Presley, Freddie Prinz, John Candy, John Belushi, Mama Cass Elliott, Jimi Hendrix, Janice Joplin, and Bob Marley have in common? They're all well-known entertainers; they're all dead; most didn't reach age 40; they all enjoyed huge financial success; and they all died of a form of substance abuse, but not always the obvious self-destructive substances such as heroin, cocaine, or prolonged use of cannabis, alcohol, and tobacco. In the deaths of John Candy and Mama Cass Elliott the lethal drug was excessive amounts of food. In other words, anything taken to excess can harm us. The key purpose in life is for each one of us to make personal choices throughout the **Six Powers of Success** and the goal is to strive to find a balance among the powers. Remember, each new day is the first day of the

rest of your life! Any power taken to excess almost always causes you to detract from one or more of the other powers.

"He who has health has hope; and he who has hope, has everything." — *Arabian Proverb*

What is it that financial advisors do? On the one hand they prospect while on the other hand they sell. These require very different skill sets.

On the left-hand side of Chart 2–2 the advisor's prospecting hand includes the five Es necessary for partnership success: energy, excitement, enthusiasm, empathy, and empowerment. The right-

---

HOLISTIC WEALTH MANAGEMENT   Chart 2–2

How Financial Advisors Do It	What Financial Advisors Do
EMPOWERMENT	**DISTRIBUTION** Transfer/Estate Planning
EMPATHY	**CONSERVATION** Spending on Lifestyle
ENTHUSIASM	**PROTECTION** Insurance/Tax Planning
EXCITEMENT	**GROWTH** Asset Allocation/ Investment Strategies
ENERGY	**ACCUMULATION** Cash Management

"I instill peace of mind by helping clients manage wealth throughout their lifecycle, to achieve and realize their dreams, and to retire with financial dignity."

---

hand side includes an overview of financial planning — the skill sets required to market and sell successfully.

The integration of these two hands will create the value-add you need from your advisor to be successful in the 21st Century.

How Many Hats Does Your Advisor Wear?

Beyond the obvious financial planning advisory skills, communication skills, and money management skills they provide, today's holistic planners are also part clergy, therapist, psychologist, marriage counsellor, family planner, executive estate consultant, and so on.

My motto when I was a stockbroker was, "I instill peace of mind by helping my clients manage wealth and wellness throughout their life cycle, to achieve and realize their dreams, and to retire with financial dignity."

My life's purpose was to empower, educate, entertain, and enlighten as many people as possible without sacrificing my personal integrity or freedom. In fact, I founded **Financial Knowledge Inc. (FKI)** to provide education for Canadians to reach the masses. The four pillars to the financial community — banks, trusts, investment dealers, and insurance companies — have been talking about educating the public for the last century, but at best they have only provided limited information; enough information to capture the sale of whatever product they are selling at the moment. Canadians require, and investors want, more than information — they need education on financial, investment, and pre-retirement planning issues. Those advisors willing to provide education and the knowledge tools to fulfill the investors' needs will be the most successful.

The Partnership Question

"If we were to meet here five years from today and you were looking back over those five years, what would have had to have happened in your personal, financial, and lifestyle pursuits for you to feel happy with your progress?"

The purpose of this question is to raise the issue of trust. Why is it so hard to trust today? I believe it is a result of what I call the 7Rs — right-sizing, right-aging, restructuring, rationalization, re-engineering, redundancies, and retentions. Corporate Canada no longer provides the paternalistic environment we used to enjoy, and the

Public Sector is moving in this direction too. Massive layoffs, delayering, mergers, acquisitions, and changing organizational structures lead us to believe that corporate loyalty no longer exists. Employee loyalty is also on the wane — it seems no one trusts anyone. Is it any wonder the three most often cited concerns in finding and developing a partnership are trust, honesty, and integrity.

Human beings spend 95% of the time on their own self-interest and only 5% on other people's interest. Your goal is to find an advisor who devotes all of his or her energy to your world. A good advisor uses many senses — visual, auditory, kinesetics (feelings) — to discover your needs, wants, objectives, feelings, and sensitivities. Using sensory acuity the advisor has the ability to make you feel like the most important person in the world. And when it comes right down to it — you are. If you feel right about this initial meeting with the advisor this can become the glue to the formation of a successful partnership.

The Role of the Advisor

All long-term studies show investors are facing information overload. What these investors need more than anything else is accurate advice. Advice is a growth business and all financial advisors are challenged today to meet their clients' needs for education and

counselling. In the process their dual goals are to focus on quality service and customer satisfaction which in reality is often stated but seldom executed.

To be successful they have to be able to address the life cycles of a client. At the heart of everything the advisor does is to build bridges of communications with other human beings. If you were to enter into a partnership with an advisor you would expect no less.

Your Personal Coach

"The quality of a person's life is in direct proportion to their commitment to excellence, regardless of their chosen field of endeavor."
— Vince Lombardi

The more successful advisors today are strengthening their client relationships by learning to become personal coaches. A competent, caring advisor will demonstrate empathy for you as a person and will be non-judgmental, nurturing, and accepting of your circumstances, unconditionally. Good interpersonal and communication skills are the most important assets to look for in a coach. Obviously, your advisor should have a great track record, lots of practical hands-on experience, and the educational requirements to go with the job. The most important qualities to look for in your coach are honesty, integrity, and loyalty which allow you to develop a trusting relationship. Without trust it will be impossible to develop a long-term meaningful partnership.

The best personal coaches utilize a holistic approach to the stewardship of finance and wealth management. They relate to their clients on all levels including physical, emotional, and spiritual wellness; lifestyle; relationships; and all aspects of the financial planning process. They integrate all ten fingers on the holistic wealth management chart and create a bonding partnership that can withstand the test of time through the life cycles of the client and the cycles of the market.

Three

To Plan or Not to Plan

FINANCIAL PLANS FAIL FOR FOUR MAIN REASONS. TWO ARE PUBLIC or government related: taxes and inflation; and two are private: procrastination and a negative mental attitude. There is not a lot you can do about taxes and inflation except to plan your affairs in the most tax-effective manner possible. Procrastination and attitude, however, are totally in your control. Of the two, procrastination has inflicted more damage, dashed more hopes and dreams, than any other trait. It is a form of self-sabotage. And only the individual can make personal choices about the role of procrastination in one's life.

In simple terms there are five reasons most people fail to achieve financial independence.

1. They do not have financial goals.
2. They do not have a cash management system.
3. They do not pay themselves first.
4. They do not plan tax savings.
5. They do not plan for risk (unexpected events).

Most Canadians do not plan to fail; they simply fail to plan. It's an old saw that is as true today as it was yesterday. So let's not delay a moment longer — let's get down to business!

How Long Should It Take You to Rehearse Your Life Plan?

It takes 1,200 hours to learn to play a flute.
It takes 900 hours to learn to sing.
It takes 1,500 hours to learn karate (black belt).

It takes 2,000 hours per year to earn a living.
So how many hours should it take to plan your retirement? The
answer is ____ hours.

In the course of our seminars I ask this question and then
invite the participants to write a single digit number between 0
and 9 in their workbooks on the right-hand side closest to hours.
Then I ask them to write the digit 4 to the left side. Each participant's workbook now includes a number that reads somewhere
between 40 and 49. Then I reveal the significance of this number
— that if they were to spend this much time rehearsing their
own life plan it would place them in the top 5% of all Canadians.
This is a shocking statistic for many, but it is reality. Some people spend 15 minutes during the last week of February at a point
of purchase display in their bank or trust company, deciding to
purchase an RRSP. Other people will spend 6 to 7 hours, donat-
ing a whole day to shopping for a new VCR or compact disc
player, to try to save $25. Yet they wouldn't spend any time at all
planning for their long-term financial and pre-retirement goals. If
you were to spend that day planning for your financial future,
the end result could be worth thousands of dollars of additional
net worth.

What is even more shocking is that in three independent surveys regarding major personal stressors — money and financial
security are always uppermost on peoples minds (see Table 3–1).
One would think that something that would cause this much
stress would be dealt with immediately, but that is not the case.
Many Canadians worry about money for their entire lives and yet
never come to grips with managing their habit of procrastination.

Surveys show that most Canadians are not adequately planning
for their futures, and they are relying too heavily on government
to provide for them in retirement. You and I know this is a false
hope. It should be obvious to you that the future is in your hands
— you and only you have the ultimate control.

Philosophy of Time

The average life expectancy for a Canadian male today is age 75;
for females it is age 81. If you have already made it to age 50
then you can add four years to both male and female ages. In the
year 1900, men could only expect to live to age 49 and women
to age 47.

MAJOR PERSONAL STRESSORS			Table 3–1
Age	18 — 34	35 — 44	45 — 54
American Management Association Middle management 2,659 polled			
Financial	71%	70%	47%
Relationships (children)	20%	43%	48%
Health	36%	36%	50%
Decima Research			
Top 3 wishes — 1,500 polled Financial security	1	3	
Youth and health	2	2	
Inner peace and happiness	3	1	
Financial Knowledge Inc. (FKI) Major concerns — 5,000 polled			
Financial		1	2
Health		2	1
Relationships		3	3

We've sure come a long way this century. Now suppose you were to retire at age 55, today; you could expect as many as 20, 30, 40 years, or more in retirement. By necessity you would need to have a very good plan. Back in the year 1900 you didn't need a plan; most people just worked until they died. In fact the average male retiring in 1997 can expect his retirement to last three times longer than the male who retired in 1967.

Now let's look at time another way. Suppose you are a male age 55 with a life expectancy of age 75. You would have 20 years left, based on an average life expectancy. This is quite a long time when we think about each year, one year at a time. Now divide the year into quarters based on the four seasons and it doesn't seem as long — 20 times to see the beautiful leaves change each fall, to see the snow come in the winter, and to see the robins return each spring. If you feel you have less time with four quarters per year, try thinking about life and longevity in terms of weeks.

"Heaven ne'er helps the man who will not act." — Sophocles

From age 55 to age 75 you would have 1,040 weeks; if you lose next week you would be down to 1,039; if you lose the following week you're down to 1,038; and so on. When you think about your life in terms of weeks you'll never want to lose another week again as long as you live. Time, you realize, is your best friend; the most precious ally you've got. Time permeates every aspect of your life throughout the six powers of success. It is obvious that time is important when we consider financial planning and compounding scenarios, but I trust you now have a healthier, more respectable notion of time as it pertains to all of the other powers in your life as well.

"To me, old age is 15 years older than I am."
— Bernard M. Baruch

PHILOSOPHY — TIME PLAN   Chart 3–2

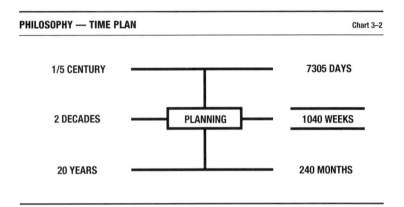

The Knowledge Economy

We have moved through three distinct economies during the past century.

1. The **agricultural** economy where wealth was land and the exchange was to barter goods.
2. The **industrial** economy where wealth was plant and equipment, labour, and capital and the exchange was paper money.
3. The **knowledge** economy where wealth is in the value of knowledge itself and the exchange is the electronic transfer of money. You can market and sell the technology via delivery systems such as ATMs, videos, TVs, VCRs, CDs, the Internet, and Electronic Data Transfers. Each transaction implies the exchange of information.

What becomes clear is that knowledge is the key core of value for the 21st century. Lifelong learning is essential to your survival. What you can't or aren't willing to learn you must purchase. The best brains are available at little or no cost when it comes to financial and investment planning. There are thousands of financial professionals waiting to help you.

Professional Help Is Available

If your family is like many of those in Canada, you may have as many as a dozen different financial "advisors" who sell or recommend dozens of different products or services.

You may have, at any one time, a banker, accountant, stockbroker, lawyer, insurance agent, and mortgage trust officer. Add your employer's benefits counsellor and your car and real estate salespeople to the list. Consider your friend who always knows what to do with money and other friends who may give you financial advice. It doesn't take long to accumulate a lengthy list of actual — and so-called — advisors.

A problem some people must face is that a number of advisors on the list will suggest variations on "entrust all your money to me and I will solve all your problems." Deep down, they know they should be carefully dividing their money among several advisors and institutions. Most people would prefer to have only one or two "trusted personal advisors" than a whole group of semi-qualified "helpers."

In the next chapter we'll take a look at all of the different types of financial intermediaries. But before we do that we should gain an understanding of how the financial planning process works.

The Six-Step Financial Planning Process

Chart 3–3 will guide you through the financial planning process. There are six steps involved in creating a formal financial plan.

Step 1: Data collection and needs assessment are first and foremost. What are your financial goals? Break these goals down into short, medium, and long-term. Short-term goals might include a car purchase, a trip, a celebration or special occasion, a renovation, or a cottage purchase. Long-term goals might include children's education plans, financial independence, retirement, and estate planning.

This stage is used to construct a series of building blocks based on your needs analysis, your core values, and where you are in the life cycle. Major segments to be discussed include your investment personality with respect to risk tolerance, time frames, relationships (spouse, children, parents), career security, present income, future income prospects, tax and estate issues, and any other major life changes.

THE SIX-STEP FINANCIAL PLANNING PROCESS   Chart 3–3

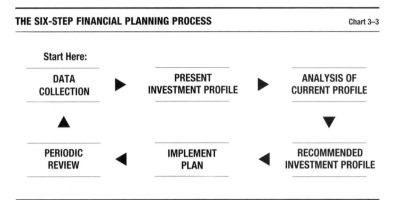

Step 2: Present investment profile is used to discover all of the facts pertaining to your current financial situation. Networth and cash flow statements are prepared to provide a snapshot of your current status. Preparation of these documents will illustrate any gap between where you are now and where you would like to be in relation to your goals.

Step 3: Analysis of current profile is used to review your current situation to see if it aligns with your goals.

Step 4: Recommended investment profile consists of a written plan with specific recommendations and details on how to achieve your goals.

Step 5: Implement plan involves processing each of the recommendations previously discussed. This stage may involve a network of other financial professionals to carry out the plan under the guidance of your financial planner who coordinates the activities of each of the other specialists.

Step 6: Periodic review should be conducted annually to reconfirm, reassess, and reactivate any old initiatives, as well as to confirm, assess, and activate new ones.

"Most of us have a pretty clear idea of the world we want, what we lack is the understanding of how to go about getting it."
— Hugh Gibson

This completes the six-step financial planning process. Adherence to your plan will help you obtain your desired result. The following can also serve as a checklist for successful financial planning:

• Stay committed to your plan.
• Communicate fully with your planner.
• Be honest with your planner.

The Six-Step Financial Planning Process

- At the data-gathering stage, provide all the information you can in complete detail.
- Don't be afraid to ask questions when you don't understand.
- At the preliminary planning stages, discuss any parts of the plan that do not reflect your situation immediately.
- As soon as you receive your financial plan, make sure you implement the recommendations right away.
- Keep your planner informed of any changes in your goals or your financial status.
- Be sure to conduct an annual financial review.

Four

Financial Service Intermediaries

MOST INVESTORS OFTEN MAKE THEIR FIRST INVESTMENT WITH AS little as a few hundred dollars at their bank or trust company. As they begin to gain knowledge they become aware of the possibility of attaining better returns with an investment advisor or financial planner. Most often they find a stockbroker or independent mutual fund advisor via a referral from family or friends. These relationships are valuable for most Canadians and can often last a lifetime. However when one reaches a more affluent status with investment assets in excess of a half million dollars, the investor will often seek out an investment counsellor who offers discretionary managed money on a flat fee or percentage of asset basis. This is not to suggest that there would be no overlaps in these broad ranges. As the banks become more competitive and hire high-profile mutual fund portfolio managers, many investors will remain with the perceived safety of the larger institution. Seasoned investors may continue to deal with their stockbrokers or mutual fund specialists, managing investment assets into the seven figures, especially since most firms offer WRAP account fee-based compensation alternatives (see Chart 4–1.)

Financial Intermediaries

Are you ready for an abbreviated version of what service each of these intermediaries provides? We'll go into much greater detail later, but for now let's take a quick tour.

Financial Planners

Financial planners are generally trained to prepare a totally comprehensive and complete financial plan. They are usually fee-based, hourly or fixed-cost, and may be licensed to sell products. They help the investor chart a course to cover all aspects of financial planning from cash management (budgeting), asset allocation and investment strategies, taxes, wills and estate plans to lifestyle and retirement issues. Financial planners normally have a Certified Financial Planner (CFP), Registered Financial Planner (RFP), or Chartered Financial Consultant (CH.F.C.) designation. If the agent does not have a recognizable designation such as CFP, RFP, or CH.F.C. then the onus is on you to question this person's qualifications to prepare your financial plan.

Mutual Fund Agents

These agents are often referred to as financial planners but more often are mutual fund specialists. Some do offer financial planning and product implementation. Some sell insurance products, and

Professional financial management reduces workload and risk.

FINANCIAL INTERMEDIARIES LIFE CYCLE Chart 4–1

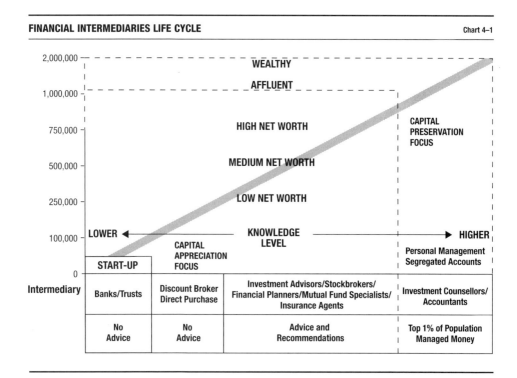

most can offer an extensive product range of GICs and many different mutual fund families. The vast majority do not have the specific training to prepare extensive financial plans however most can provide investment advice. Most mutual fund agents represent a full range of mutual fund families, however, some are single-family agents restricted to selling only their employer's product line.

Stockbrokers

Securities brokers offer full service on the widest range of products of all intermediaries. Traditionally paid on a commission basis, some brokers are now switching to a flat fee basis. When licensed by the provincial securities commission after passing the Canadian securities course, a broker can act as an advisor. The highest designation in this profession is Fellow of the Canadian Securities Institute (FCSI) which involves several major courses on all aspects of financial planning. Stockbrokers share responsibility for investment decisions with the investor. A broker's full range of products include money market instruments, bonds, stocks, options, derivatives, and mutual funds. Some brokers specialize in one or two areas, others offer the full range.

Investment Counsellors

Counsellors are relatively unknown to most Canadians. However there are a few dozen firms that offer investment services to high net worth individuals and institutions. Minimum account size is usually over $500,000 but a few firms offer services for accounts of $100,000 or more. Their only business is to manage portfolios and advise individual clients. Most consellors have a Chartered Financial Analyst (CFA) designation.

The investor's separately managed or segregated account is established with a money manager who, at the outset, will focus on your needs such as risk tolerance, goals, and objectives. Once established the investor empowers the money manager to manage the assets at the counsellor's discretion.

Insurance Agents

Most agents specialize in life and disability insurance products, and many are licensed to sell mutual funds. They are usually limited to one mutual fund family product line; however some offer multiple families of funds and segregated funds. Many agents obtain the Chartered Life Underwriter (CLU) or Chartered Financial Consultant (CH.F.C.), which enables the agent to provide more extensive financial planning applications with a client, but most are not specifically trained as financial planners.

Accountants

Most accountants offer tax planning, business structure advice, and high net worth individual counselling. For the most part they are not financial planners, nor do they provide investment advice or financial products. Two common designations for the accounting profession include Certified General Accountant (CGA) and Chartered Accountant (CA).

Direct Purchase — No-Load

The boomer generation is part of the do-it-yourself revolution willing to experiment and try things on their own. A number of independent mutual fund companies bypass the traditional agency arrangement of accepting orders from brokers, advisors, dealers, or planners. Instead investors can deal directly with the individual mutual fund company and pay no commissions when buying or selling. Some mutual fund companies charge a nominal start-up fee, usually $40 or $50, to cover administration costs. This is a token amount when you consider the overall savings.

Banks and Trusts

In the span of two decades, banks have made their presence felt by capturing a major part of the mutual fund industry and the control of the major investment dealers. Banks have also been busy acquiring trust companies and insurance affiliates on their road to one-stop shopping for Canadian consumers. But it is not all roses. Many Canadians find their myriad of fees for services offensive and feel gouged by credit card rates and service charges while banks report billion dollar profits.

"The memory strengthens as you lay burdens on it, and becomes trustworthy as you trust it."
— Thomas De Quincey

Know more about your choices

Canadians love to hate banks, and yet every February, at the peek of the RRSP season, they line up to buy mutual funds from the intermediary they trust the most. Most bank-sponsored mutual funds underperform the industry averages year after year. Yet Canadians, knowingly or not, continue to choose the bank or trust company that they visit once or twice a month as their line of least resistance.

Discount Brokers

Banks have emerged as the major source for discount brokerage services. Along with their full-service brokerage affiliates, they offer a deep-discount, no frills option for sophisticated investors who can make their own decisions. But are these investors really better off selecting this option? Evidence proves that some investors are; however, many are not. The Bank of Canada publishes quarterly statistics that show the flow of cash between money market funds, bond funds, and equity funds. Inevitably the major swings to buy or sell within these three sectors take place at the wrong time in the market cycle. The message here is to know yourself, especially your temperament, as to how you will react when the inevitable market gyrations occur.

For those who have the business acumen and the skill set to manage on their own, the rewards can be great. Discounts can be as large as 85% on some stock transactions and acquisition costs for mutual funds are 2% or lower, based on the size or dollar value of the trade. Even deeper discounts are available to those investors who enter trades on their personal computers via modem, using special software provided by their broker.

Major Discount Brokers

Discount Broker	*Owned By*
Green Line Investor Services	Toronto-Dominion Bank
Investor's Edge	CIBC
Scotia Discount Brokerage	Bank of Nova Scotia
Action Direct Inc.	Royal Bank of Canada
InvestorLine	Bank of Montreal
CT Market Partner	Canada Trustco Ltd.
Hongkong Bank Discount Trading Inc.	Hongkong Bank of Canada

Deep Discount Mutual Fund Dealers

A small group of deep discount fund dealers offer load funds at no cost. Through these discounters it is possible to access the top performing independent funds with no front-end acquisition costs or any costs on redemption. These discounters make their money from the annual trailer fees paid to them by the fund companies in return for managing their clients' funds. These fees typically range from 0.15% to 1% of the assets under management, are part of the dealer compensation costs, and are paid from the management fees charged to each fund. This is an indirect cost that is not visible to the investor. These service fees, which are paid to all brokers, do not get charged to your account, nor do they result in higher management fees.

Financial Intermediaries Summary

The financial planning industry is experiencing an exponential growth curve which should continue for the next two decades. You owe it to yourself to learn what each of these financial service providers can and can't do for you. Beware of so-called assorted specialists without credentials — ask specifically what degrees and designations they have and which memberships they hold within the financial services community. This topic will be discussed in more depth in Chapter 5 The Educational Edge.

Work Smarter — Not Harder

With the proliferation of multiple products available today and the myriad of options to choose from, how does the investor find the time to cope and still make prudent investments. The decision should be taken at the outset of establishing a financial plan and/or an investment portfolio. The question the investor needs to ask is, "How much time am I really willing to spend on my financial affairs?" The answer to this question should tell you what strengths you bring to the table. Most investors realize that in order to simplify their lives they need an advisor who can alleviate much of the **hard work**. As well today, most advisors use sophisticated software for financial planning and portfolio analysis, which allows them to create customized investment models for their clients. Reduced paperwork, higher technology, computerized modules, and communications technology allow your advisor to **work smarter** thereby freeing up more of your time to pursue other interests.

Could You Manage Your Own Financial Plan?

"No train, no pain, no strain, no gain!" — Graydon Watters Although managing your portfolio can be a time-consuming task, rest assured you don't need a post-graduate degree to do well with your investments. In fact some successful investors never graduated from high school. All it really takes is common sense, the right information, and a lot of time and interest.

You have already demonstrated your financial common sense and interest by reading this book. You are well on your way to acquiring the practical knowledge and skills needed to manage your portfolio. But do you have the time?

Time — Do you have the time to read financial papers and investment reports after work? How many evenings do you wish to devote to learning, aside from the time you are already investing in this course? Is your interest in financial planning genuine enough to see you through the time and work necessary to learn the concepts?

Training — Do you have training in accounting, economics, cycles, investments, and statistical analysis required for success in devising a financial plan? Are you willing to pursue this type of learning at this stage of your life?

Temperament — Do you have the "stomach" to rely on your own decisions in serious financial matters? Not all investment decisions are clear cut. Are you comfortable making decisions in a "gray" zone with incomplete knowledge?

Money — Do you have adequate investment resources of your own to build a diversified portfolio suitable to your personal comfort level?

To discover whether you have the time, training, temperament, and money to manage your financial planning entirely on your own, complete the exercise in Table 4–2. Be very candid about your situation as you rate yourself in each of these areas. Circle the number that reflects your true position. When you're finished, add all the points circled, and read the interpretation of your total score.

PROFESSIONAL MANAGEMENT VERSUS SELF-MANAGEMENT					Table 4–2
	Professional Management			**Self-Management**	
Time	0	1	2	3	4	5
Knowledge	0	1	2	3	4	5
Temperament	0	1	2	3	4	5
Money	0	1	2	3	4	5
Score: _____					

Scoring

17 — 20 points

You've got what it takes to manage your financial plan. You know how to set goals and implement investment strategies to fulfill your needs and objectives.

12 — 16 points

You are well on your way. You know what your goals are, but you are not sure about implementing them on your own. You require the services of an investment advisor or a financial planner who understands your needs and objectives. Your investment strategies may take a self-managed approach with professional guidance from your investment advisor, or it may include professionally managed mutual funds.

0 — 11 points

You, along with 90% of investors, should consider professional money management. You need help in establishing your goals, and you require the assistance of an investment advisor, a mutual fund specialist, a financial planner, or other financial professional to implement your plan. A combination of adequate reserves to match your selection of professionally managed mutual funds will allow you to accomplish your investment objectives and provide you with financial independence in the future.

Financial Knowledge Inc. (FKI) conducts ongoing surveys with the participants in our programs. A survey completed during 1997, covering in excess of 1000 participants, revealed the data in Table 4–3, regarding professional versus self-management.

"I not only use all the brains that I have, but all that I can borrow."
— Woodrow Wilson

Do you have the time and financial knowledge?

FKI PARTICIPANTS SURVEY — PROFESSIONAL VERSUS SELF-MANAGEMENT						Table 4–3
	Professional Management			Self-Management		
	0	1	2	3	4	5
Time	27%	24%	27%	7%	10%	5%
Training	22%	32%	20%	17%	5%	4%
Temperament	12%	34%	20%	12%	17%	5%
Money	12%	34%	10%	27%	12%	5%

As you can see from this survey the vast majority of the participants require professional help and need to seek the services of an investment advisor for the following reasons:

78% do not have the time to manage their money.
74% do not have the training or knowledge.
66% do not have the temperament to make timing decisions.
56% do not have adequate financial capital to diversify.

Five

The Educational Edge

WE LIVE IN AN ERA WHEN VIRTUALLY ANYONE CAN HANG A SHINGLE and claim to be a financial planner. Historically the financial service industry has been unregulated and, while there have been attempts to regulate it more recently, there is still a lot of disagreement and much lobbying as to how and who should perform this task. Many planners and advisors have a series of initials following their names and it's important for you to know what these degrees or designations represent in terms of expertise and training. What's in a name? A lot — much more than you might think!

Formal Education — Credentials

Although a graduate degree is not required many financial professionals have university degrees with a concentration in finance, economics, accounting, marketing, computers, investments, psychology, and human resources.

In addition the top financial professionals will have earned specialty industry designations: A financial planner will have a Certified Financial Planner (CFP) or Registered Financial Planner (RFP); a stockbroker or financial advisor will be a Fellow of the Canadian Securities Institute (FCSI). As well, financial professionals should have memberships in their industry trade associations such as the Canadian Association of Financial Planners (CAFP), Financial Planners Standards Council of Canada (FPSCC), Canadian Association of Pre-retirement Planners (CAPP), and the FCSI mentioned above. Beyond a university degree, a designation, and a membership in an industry association, the financial professional ideally has several years of hands-on practical business experience.

Financial Service Industry Designations

There are numerous designations that lend credibility to qualifying your choice of a financial professional. The most common designations for each financial services intermediary are as follows:

Financial Planners: Certified Financial Planner (CFP) and Registered Financial Planner (RFP)
Mutual Fund Agents: Basic mutual fund courses offered by the Investment Funds Institute of Canada (IFIC)
Stockbrokers: Fellow of the Canadian Securities Institute (FCSI)
Investment Counsellors: Chartered Financial Analyst (CFA)
Insurance Agents: Chartered Financial Consultant (CH.F.C.) and Chartered Life Underwriter (CLU)
Direct Purchase No-Load: None
Banks and Trust: Personal Financial Counselling (PFC) and Personal Financial Planning (PFP)
Discount Brokers: None

Other common designations and/or university degrees that planners or advisors might have earned are

Certified Public Accountant (CPA)
Certified General Accountant (CGA)
Chartered Accountant (CA)
Bachelor of Commerce (B. Comm,)
Bachelor of Science (B. Sc.)
Bachelor of Engineering (B. Eng.)
Masters of Business Administration (MBA)

It is not uncommon to meet a person who holds two or three designations acquired over the years while engaged in other occupations. The financial service industry is currently one of the greatest growth industries and will be for the foreseeable future. While many industries were downsizing, restructuring, or re-engineering during the last several years, the financial service industry has doubled in size, attracting many new people with many different facets of practical experience and very diverse backgrounds.

Financial Planners Standards Council of Canada (FPSCC)

It has become an absolute minefield for the typical investor to sort out who's who in the financial planning industry when anyone and everyone can use the term financial planner. Enter the Financial Planners Standards Council of Canada. The board is made up of several associations that deal with the personal finances of individuals. The FPSCC is working actively with regulators towards the principle that one organization should set the standards for the financial planning industry. This dovetails with the goal of the Ontario Securities Commission Investment Funds Steering Group, the Stromberg Report, whereby all financial planning participants should be required to commit to set standards.

The FPSCC has an ongoing awareness program to educate the public to recognize the Certified Financial Planner (CFP) designation as the competency and ethical standard against which all financial planners should be measured. There are currently 3,000 CFPs in Canada and this number is expected to double by 1998.

The major benefit for the layperson and the consumer of financial products is that the FPSCC will only issue the internationally recognized CFP degree to those who meet strict standards of education, examination, experience, and ethics. To qualify, a financial planner or advisor must complete several university equivalent courses with several assignments and final examinations over a minimum period of 18 months. After receiving the CFP designation a planner or advisor must earn 30 hours of continuing education credits to stay abreast of changes in the profession.

FPSCC — Code of Ethics

The seven principles of the FPSCC Code of Ethics recognize the individual CFP designee's responsibilities to the public, clients, colleagues, employers, and to the profession. They apply to all CFP designees and provide guidance to them in the performance of their professional services.

Integrity: A CFP designee shall offer and provide professional services with integrity.

Objectivity: A CFP designee shall be objective in providing professional services to clients.

Competence: A CFP designee shall provide services to clients competently and maintain the necessary knowledge and skill to continue to do so in those areas in which the designee is engaged.

Fairness: A CFP designee shall perform professional services in a manner that is fair and reasonable to clients, principals, partners, and employers and shall disclose conflict(s) of interest in providing such services.

Confidentiality: A CFP designee shall maintain confidentiality of all client information.

Professionalism: A CFP designee's conduct in all matters shall reflect credit upon the profession.

Diligence: A CFP designee shall act diligently in providing professional services.

Canadian Securities Institute (CSI)

CANADIAN SECURITIES INSTITUTE

This non-profit organization is sponsored by the Investment Dealers Association and Canada's stock exchanges. They offer two educational programs leading to the CFP designation: the Canadian Securities Course and the Professional Financial Planning Course. All newly licensed brokerage representatives must complete the PFPC within 30 months of being licensed.

The Institute also sponsors the Investment Learning Centre, a non-profit organization that provides information to the public about investing. The Centre also offers investment seminars for the public.

Fellow of the Canadian Securities Institute (FCSI)

There are just under 3,000 FCSIs in Canada today, but this number is expected to increase substantially over the next few years. Originally offered to stockbrokers and investment advisors, the FCSI designation is now available to all professionals who qualify. The collapse of the four pillars of finance created greater similarities among the professions. The goal of the Canadian Securities Institute (CSI) was to create a designation for financial professionals from any pillar of the financial services industry.

In order for FCSIs to be recognized by Canadian investors as the country's premier investment advisors, the CSI has adopted very tough entry standards, including completion of the Canadian Securities Course (CSC). Candidates must have written the Conduct and Practices exam and must have taken any course leading to Canadian Investment Management I (CIM I) plus Canadian

Investment Management II (CIM II) and Canadian Investment Finance. As well each candidate for the FCSI designation must

- have five years' work experience in the financial services industry, within the last eight years
- obtain an endorsement from a FCSI, a letter from his/her employer, and present a candidate's letter of intent
- take ongoing education based on points schedule
- be regulated by National Council of FCSIs, which has the power to propose that a membership be revoked in certain circumstances

FCSI — Code of Professional Ethics

Some of the qualities held by the FCSI are excellence, dedication, integrity, and trust. The designation of FCSI is hard won through new standards more rigorous than any ever adopted which include long years of proven exceptional service, advanced academic achievement, and the highest standards of ethical conduct.

Investment Funds Institute of Canada (IFIC)

Most of Canada's mutual fund companies and distributors are represented by IFIC. They offer a home study course which is a minimum requirement for licensing to sell mutual funds in Canada. The course teaches basic financial planning and asset allocation strategies. Beware of the person who has met the basic requirements to sell mutual funds but has no depth of practical experience or financial planning knowledge. Many agents who call themselves financial planners have not met the formal requirements nor do they have the experience to justify using that title.

Canadian Institute of Financial Planning (CIFP)

This non-profit organization is sponsored by the Investment Funds Institute of Canada (IFIC). Their program consists of six courses with four assignments each and a final exam. I can assure you that anyone who attains the CFP designation has put in some hard work. The six courses would compare with a complete year of university. Many who attempt the program fail to complete it because of the difficulty — especially the course on taxation. IFIC is currently developing a continuing education program for its members based on three tracks:

1. **Mutual fund track** will specialize in mutual funds, asset allocation modules, portfolio management, theory, and practice.
2. **Financial planning track** will adapt the existing six courses offered by the CIFP to both mutual fund specialists and financial planners.
3. **General track** will focus on practice management and client relationship skills.

Canadian Association of Financial Planners (CAFP)

This Association has historically offered both the Chartered Financial Planner (CFP) and Registered Financial Planner (RFP) designations. With the newly formed Financial Planners Standards Council of Canada (FPSCC) offering the Certified Financial Planner (CFP) designation, controversy evolved over the professional use of the letters CFP. Because the Certified Financial Planners designation had been registered and used internationally in the United States, Japan, Australia, New Zealand, and the United Kingdom it made sense for Canada to adopt to the FPSCCs designation. All of the existing Chartered Financial Planners have been grandfathered into the new Certified Financial Planners with industry-wide standards that the public can identify.

Perhaps the highest standard a financial planner can attain is the Registered Financial Planner (RFP) designation. RFPs are the most disciplined, well trained, and highly regulated of all financial planners. They must carry mandatory Errors and Omissions Insurance and obtain 30 hours of continuing education each year. There are only about 500 RFPs in Canada. Any person who carries this designation is definitely serious about the profession.

RFPs must have a university degree in commerce or finance, must write a comprehensive six-hour exam, must be a CAFP member for one year, must be in practice for two years, must be sponsored by three other CAFP members, must complete a sample plan to be judged by senior members of the CAFP, and must uphold standards of professional conduct and ethics.

Life Underwriters Association of Canada (LUAC)

This association sets conduct, ethics, and professional development standards for life and health insurance agents. They provide courses for 18,000 members, specializing in financial and estate planning issues and all aspects of risk management. To become an insurance agent one must take a life insurance course, which leads to provincial licensing exams. If, in addition, the agent wants to sell securities and provide financial services he or she must enroll in the CFP courses. Two high quality professional designations available to life insurance agents are the Chartered Financial Consultant (CH.F.C.) and the Chartered Life Underwriter (CLU). The CH.F.C. provides advanced training in wealth accumulation and retirement planning. The CLU provides specialty training in life and health insurance and group benefits for employees. LUAC has conduct and ethics standards and continuing education requirements, which must be maintained.

Institute of Canadian Bankers (ICB)

Since deregulation all banks have been developing counter personnel to provide basic financial planning services and product advice to customers. Bankers coined the phrase "relationship banking" to enhance their marketing efforts, particularly with respect to packaged proprietary products such as mutual funds. Bank employees are encouraged to enroll in courses offered by the ICB to earn the Personal Financial Counselling (PFC) or Personal Financial Planning (PFP) designations. the PFC designation requires four courses on basic financial planning needs and objectives of clients, while the PFP consists of five courses of more advanced material to serve clients with more complex needs.

Three Prestigious Designations

By adopting nation-wide standards Canadians will be able to choose a financial professional with confidence. Individuals seeking in-depth financial planning would most often choose a Certified Financial Planner (CFP) or Registered Financial Planner (RFP). Others seeking in-depth investment advice including asset allocation, investment selection, and portfolio management strategies might choose a Fellow of the Canadian Securities Institute (FCSI).

There are numerous other designations to consider when evaluating a financial advisor's capabilities and expertise.

Chartered Accountant (CA), Chartered Financial Analyst (CFA), or a person who has a Masters of Business Administration (MBA) would have had to complete a very tough program to earn the right to use those initials. As an investor you need to know the educational background of the advisor, what degrees and/or designations he or she has, what specialty areas he or she covers, and if he or she meets your needs and requirements.

How Do Your Current Advisors Measure Up?

How would you rate each of the many advisors you currently use? What designations do they have? How well do they communicate with you? Does the chemistry feel right? How would you rate their listening skills? Are they truly empathetic and responsive to your personal situation and needs? These are just a few of the questions you might want to ask yourself. You may find the exercise in Worksheet 5–1 valuable in measuring the strengths of your existing advisory relationships and in understanding where you may need professional assistance.

ADVISOR RATING CHECKLIST						Worksheet 5–1
	Don't Have	Poor	Good	Very Good	Excellent	Degree/ Designations
Financial Planner	❏	❏	❏	❏	❏	_____
Mutual Fund Agent	❏	❏	❏	❏	❏	_____
Stockbroker	❏	❏	❏	❏	❏	_____
Investment Counsellor	❏	❏	❏	❏	❏	_____
Insurance Agent	❏	❏	❏	❏	❏	_____
Accountant	❏	❏	❏	❏	❏	_____
Direct Purchase No-Load	❏	❏	❏	❏	❏	_____
Bank or Trust Officer	❏	❏	❏	❏	❏	_____
Discount Broker	❏	❏	❏	❏	❏	_____

The Buck Stops With You

Whatever route you choose still involves you. Your responsibility to yourself is to become an active participant. You must acquire as much knowledge as possible about financial planning each and every year so that between now and your retirement you will have the necessary knowledge tools to enjoy a financially secure, worry-free retirement.

You could start by regularly reading a financial paper like *The Financial Post*, and subscribing to one or two newsletters. Purchase self-help books; tune in to a weekly radio talk show or a TV program such as Louis Rukeyser's *Wall Street Week*; attend public seminars and listen to the gurus; request and read several annual reports, mutual fund prospectuses, and financial literature; finally, attend community college courses. With all of this newly acquired knowledge will come power when you take action.

As you grow and learn you'll know the questions to ask of your advisor; you'll be able to talk the same language. With knowledge you'll have the confidence to know if your advisor is the right person for you; if the chemistry is there to form a partnership.

"Destiny is not a matter of chance, it is a matter of choice."
— Anonymous

There are many ways to choose a financial advisor. Always start with qualifications — the alphabet soup of initials that follow their names. Verify who they work for and their regulatory and professional networks affiliations.

Six

Fees, Commissions, Loads, and Trailers

PRIOR TO DEREGULATION IN THE MID-1980S THE FOUR PILLARS OF the financial community stood distinctly, and the investor knew exactly how much he or she had to pay for services rendered. Banks and trust companies charged fees, while investment brokers and insurance agents charged commissions. Today, the four pillars are no longer distinct; they have merged, strategically aligned, networked, taken-over, or otherwise consolidated their businesses. Now most offer a full range of both fee and commission services. The most notable change since deregulation has been the astronomical growth in the mutual fund industry from $4 billion in assets in 1982 to over $250 billion in mid-1997.

There is a trend today away from commissions and towards fee-only planning. This compensation trend is very beneficial for the investor because it ensures financial professionals are offering a service rather than marketing a commodity. The investor should be aware, however, there are different ways of charging fees. A true fee-only planner is paid purely by fees, and a commission-based advisor is paid commission on the products sold to the investor. Some planners/advisors charge fees and commissions and are known as fee-based or fee-offset planners/advisors. They charge a fee for planning and then charge commissions on the investments recommended in their plan.

Financial Service Compensation Surveys

Our surveys indicate that most investors prefer fees over commissions. Flat fee or fees based on assets under management result in higher client satisfaction. Investors imply they have a greater level of trust with fee-based advisors. Commission-driven product sales, front-end or back-end loads, and trailer commissions from mutual fund management companies are often viewed negatively.

"The world does not pay for what a person knows. But it pays for what a person does with what he knows."
— Lawrence Lee

Are fees really better than commissions? What would prevent a planner from charging 2% of the net asset value of assets under management and then providing virtually no service at all; or billing a client for 12 hours when only 6 hours were actually required. Moreover, a planner who claims to be fee-based could charge fees and commissions as well as receiving trailers from the mutual fund companies. It is human nature to be biased and somewhat cynical about a profession that manages money and wealth which is so dear to our hearts. **I don't believe one method of compensation is better than another. However, some planners are inherently better than others and their method of compensation doesn't dictate their results.** Perhaps the more important issue regardless of how planners are paid is to disclose to the client in writing how they will be compensated. The client has the right to know exactly what he or she is paying for.

Free Preliminary Consultation

A no pressure, non-judgmental, get acquainted session is what most investors would like to experience in their first meeting with an advisor. There should be absolutely no mention of products at this session. Rather this is the opportunity for both parties to feel each other out, to get to know one another, to see if the chemistry is right.

To establish the initial meeting with an advisor it is best to conduct a short telephone interview with several candidates for a period of 7 to 10 minutes. Does the chemistry feel right? Is the advisor empathetic and compatible? You will know whether you will want to meet this person face-to-face at the conclusion of your mini interview. Here is a sampling of the types of questions you should ask during the telephone interview:

- What are your qualifications, professional experience, and credentials?
- What degrees, designations and industry memberships do you have?

- What types of products and areas of specialization do you provide?
- How are you compensated — commissions, fees, or both?

These are just a few of the questions you can ask to qualify the advisor by telephone. A more extensive questionnaire entitled *How To Choose A Financial Advisor* is included in Chapter 13 and can be used in your initial face-to-face interview.

To Load or Not to Load

The mutual fund industry has created so many different pricing structures that it has become almost impossible for the average investor to keep informed. In fact many people working in the financial services industry can't keep abreast of the myriad of pricing options. Mutual funds offer two varieties "load or no-load" options to purchase. Most load funds are sold by stockbrokers, advisors, or financial planners. No-load funds are usually sold directly to the investor by the management company, independent fund managers, trust companies, and banks. An investor can purchase front-load, back-load, low-load, or no-load, and virtually all funds have trailer fees. This could be looked at from the dealers perspective as you can pay me now, pay me later, or pay me always!

"The man who will use his skill and constructive imagination to see how much he can give for a dollar, instead of how little he can give for a dollar is bound to succeed."
— Henry Ford

The responsibility to communicate full and complete disclosure as to compensation for verbal or written financial planning advice and/or product implementation rests with the planner/advisor.

Historically most financial planners were fee-based and most financial advisors were commission driven. It is not uncommon for a planner or an advisor to work for both fees and commissions. And where mutual funds form part of the investor's portfolio the planner/advisor could receive trailer fees from the mutual fund management company as well.

The question each investor must ask is whether **to load or not to load**. Major studies have shown that both load and no-load funds have similar performances over one-, three-, and five-year time frames in Canada; and that no-loads have consistently outperformed load funds on average in the United States. Investors who have the time, energy, knowledge, and temperament to aggressively seek out no-load investment products might save a little money; those who don't might have to pay a little

Can you manage your own financial plan?

more, depending on how well they negotiate for the services of their financial intermediary. However, while it may be slightly cheaper to manage your own account, studies have shown that most no-load, no-advice investors' portfolios do not perform as well as those managed by financial professionals. Why? Because people who manage their own accounts often make buy and sell decisions at precisely the wrong time based on emotion, panic, and over-reaction to media coverage.

Front-End Load Funds

The traditional compensation method for the sale of mutual funds was a commission charge paid by the investor to the dealer. Historically these rates varied between 2% to 9%, depending on a number of factors such as the size of the transaction. Today negotiable commissions ranging from 0% to 5% are the norm on most transactions.

Many fund companies offer several different types of funds within their family so that the investor can diversify holdings. Most mutual fund companies allow switching privileges within their family at between 0% to 2%, and these are negotiable with your dealer.

Recent statistics have shown an increase in load funds ending a trend that saw load funds losing market share to no-load rivals. The sheer size of the industry with the proliferation of products and options available is too much for the average investor to handle. This information overload scenario is causing individual investors to turn to brokers, advisors, and planners for advice on which funds to buy. Most full-service brokers and planners will negotiate front-end loads of 1% to 3%, depending on the size and value of the account. Some will even charge 0%, relying exclusively on service or trailer fees. Whenever an investor can negotiate a 2% or lower front-end load, it is usually the best option to take.

Back-End Redemption Funds

Commission paid on redemption of mutual funds, often referred to as a deferred sales charge (DSC), is the most popular payment choice of today's investors. Why? First because most advisors suggest this method so they can compete with the no-load fund competition, and second they rationalize that if you hold the mutual fund investment long term there will be no cost (see Chart 6–1.)

Buyers should be cautious of back-end redemptions in a few areas.

- You are captive for several years and pay commissions on a declining scale each year often starting at 5.5% to 6% and remaining in a high range of 4% to 5% for the first few years.
- On redemption you might pay on the original amount invested or current market value; if it's the latter you could pay substantially more than you expected.
- You could be subject to an increased management fee of an extra 0.25% to 0.5%, which, even over a short period of time, could be greater than you would have paid on a front-end load.

Consider this data with the fact that most Canadians hold their mutual fund investments just over two years even though in theory they are meant to be held longer term. This sure makes a good case for reconsidering a front-load option, especially today when commissions are negotiable. Brokers and planners rarely charge more than 4% to 5%, and many will negotiate 1% to 3% or lower, depending upon the size of the transaction.

A common privilege for the back-end redemption option allows investors to redeem up to 10% of the aggregate net asset value of the funds they own with no penalty.

TYPICAL REDEMPTION SCHEDULE	Table 6–1
If Redeemed During the Following Periods Redemption Charge After Date of Issue	**Percentage**
1st year	5.5
2nd year	5.5
3rd year	4.5
4th year	4.0
5th year	3.5
6th year	2.5
7th year	1.5
thereafter	Nil

No-Load and Low-Load Funds

No-load funds better known as no advice, no service funds are offered by the major banks and trust companies, other deposit taking institutions, and a number of independent fund companies. A common misconception is that these funds perform better than load funds. Nothing could be further from the truth. There are more first quartile performers among the load funds than the no-load group.

A recent study by Portfolio Analytics compared load and no-load management expense ratios (MER) and found that no-loads had a lower MER overall, 1.56% versus 1.95% for load funds. And yet long term more load funds have outperformed no-load funds. Other factors that affect the MER are

- managerial styles and risk/reward approaches to those styles have a bearing on the final results
- load funds tend to buy more loyalty
- no-load bank funds typically attract inexperienced and price conscious investors who inevitably make bad decisions at major market timing points

The major argument given by no-load supporters is that sales commissions inflate the management expense ratio and are charged to the mutual fund assets therefore lowering the overall performance of the fund. Load fund advocates counter that no-load funds must spend substantially more money on advertising and distribution fees to attract buyers, which also lowers their fund performance. In the final analysis neither load nor no-load funds is a clear winner in the battle for performance.

Another group of funds offered with a low-load option gives the investor another choice. These funds are considered attractive because, with lower loads, they are deemed to perform better. Once again, "you get what you pay for." There is no hard evidence that these funds outperform their rivals. In fact some low-load and no-load funds often provide dealers with fatter service or trailer fees, which will affect a fund's performance in all future years that you own the fund. In the final analysis, fees should be secondary to choosing the best performing funds and the managerial style that suits your investment needs.

Trailer Fees

All unit holders of mutual funds pay trailer fees which are a built-in cost of the monthly management fees that fund companies charge against the assets under management. Brokers, agents, planners, and other representatives who sell the funds receive these trailers indefinitely until the funds are sold. Depending on the type of fund, the trailer ranges from 0.25% to 1% per year. Over time this can add up to a substantial amount as can be seen in Table 6–2.

TRAILER AMOUNT				Table 6–2
	FRONT END LOAD EQUIVALENT %			
Years held	0.25%	0.50%	0.75%	1.00%
1	0.25	0.50	0.76	1.01
2	0.50	1.01	1.52	2.03
3	0.75	1.52	2.28	3.06
4	1.01	2.03	3.06	4.10
5	1.26	2.54	3.84	5.15
10	2.53	5.14	7.82	10.57
15	3.83	7.81	11.95	16.27
20	5.13	10.54	16.25	22.26

If you were to total the trailer fees year to year what would you have paid if we equated this trailer fee to a front-end load option? Assuming the trailer fee was 0.75% annually and the fund was held for 10 years this would equal 7.82%. Assume further an investment of $10,000 where the investor negotiates a 2% front-end load. The total invested would be $9,800 net, which equals a 2.04% load. When added to the 7.82% trailer the total outlay for advice and service is 9.86% or a simple average of 0.986% or just under 1% per year.

Trailers were designed to encourage advisors to look after clients on an ongoing basis. The problem is that not all advisors actually provide service to their clients for this fee. Glorianne Stromberg, the OSC Commissioner, in her report on the mutual fund industry felt that investors need to have a better understanding of how these fees are charged, the impact they have on management, and what they are receiving for the trailer fees they pay.

Brokers, dealers, and planners argue that trailers provide the following benefits to investors:

- They prevent active turnover — jumping from fund to fund to boost commissions.
- They promote a managed approach and the advisor has a direct stake in your welfare — the better the fund performs the greater the trailer.
- They compensate the advisor for ongoing service — never begrudge a professional his/her due.
- They allow investors to negotiate substantial discounts on front-end load options because of the additional compensation the agent will receive.

In the final analysis the investor simply needs to know what he or she is receiving for what he or she is paying. A written agreement outlining all methods of compensation between the broker and the investor would be the ideal. This greater accountability will reward the agents who truly bring value-added benefits to the equation.

Management Fees

We are often asked the question, "If I buy a no-load mutual fund, how does the manager get paid?" Most investors don't realize how mutual fund companies are structured. Generally the fund is set up as a trust or a corporation owned by the unit holders or shareholders and run by a board of directors. Each mutual fund company hires a manager or committee to make investment

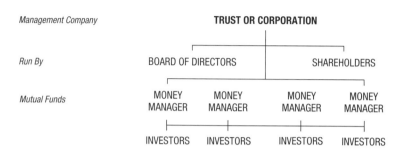

Management Company	**TRUST OR CORPORATION**			
Run By	BOARD OF DIRECTORS		SHAREHOLDERS	
Mutual Funds	MONEY MANAGER	MONEY MANAGER	MONEY MANAGER	MONEY MANAGER
	INVESTORS	INVESTORS	INVESTORS	INVESTORS

decisions for the fund. The manager may also act as the distributor that markets the fund and maintains the client records.

Each of the mutual fund managers or committees must be compensated for their efforts. They charge an annual management fee against the net asset value of the fund based on one-twelfth of a year and paid monthly. Management fees are based on the type of asset under management and vary widely.

How much should you pay your personal money manager?

Management Fees (Average)

Money market	0.25% — 0.75%
Bonds	1.00% — 2.00%
Balanced	1.25% — 2.25%
Equity	2.00% — 3.00%

Management Expense Ratio (MER)

This ratio is determined by accounting for the cost of operating the fund and is expressed as a percentage of the net assets of the fund. The MER is calculated by adding the management fees as well as other expenses charged to the fund, including operating and administration expenses such as legal, custodial, safekeeping, accounting costs, and trailer fees. Excluded from the MER calculation are brokerage commissions, interest charges, and taxes.

The importance of the MER to the investor is the lower the ratio the better the value of the fund. Generally funds with a high MER do not perform as well as those with a lower ratio. Over a long period of time this can amount to substantial dollars.

In the following example Fund A invests $4,000 annually for 25 years at 10% and has a MER of 2.5%. Now assume Fund B could produce a similar return to Fund A, but with a 1% lower MER. Result: the extra 1% per annum would translate into an extra $75,280 in value-added performance. That additional 1% is equivalent to almost 19 years of your capital contributions (19 years x $4,000 = $76,000).

RRSP Annual

Fund	Contribution	MER	Years	% Return	Total
A	$4,000	2.50%	25	10%	$432,720
B	$4,000	1.50%	25	11%	$508,000
Variance		1.00%			$75,280

Generally, MERs are higher in Canada than in the United States. Some analysts have predicted much lower Canadian rates here in the future; however, it is doubtful that Canadian MERs will ever be as low as those in the U.S. for several reasons.

- Canadian demographics are substantially smaller — a much smaller population means less economies of scale.

- Canadian investors are not as cost conscious — many don't even know how much they pay.
- Brokers and planners will continue to recommend the higher load funds, which provide their bread and butter.
- There is a heavier burden of regulation across multiple provincial jurisdictions in Canada.

Full-Service Brokerage Firms

Since the deregulation of securities commissions in 1986, brokerage companies have operated to a grid that is not available to the public. The grids can have many variations, but in general trades under $5,000 in value tend to be very expensive relative to discount brokers, and trades below $1,000 are often penalized with minimum commissions of 7% to 8% on a one-way purchase. However, these transactions can often be negotiated.

As the transaction size increases, costs come down substantially — a $10,000 trade might attract a commission of 1.4% to 1.8%, whereas a $50,000 trade might range from 0.7% to 1.2%. Keep in mind that these rates can be negotiated at most firms, depending upon your relationship with the broker. If your broker won't negotiate rates with you then you should assess the other value-added benefits he or she is providing to merit your business.

Independant salespeople can offer you a
wider selection of investment products

Consumers will be the ultimate winners as the level playing field continues to adjust over the next few years. With discount brokers charging $30 for smaller trades, Internet trading available for $20 or less per transaction, and some public companies willing to offer their shares directly to the public at discounts to market price, the full-service broker will have to offer more value-added services to their clients to remain competitive.

Wrap Accounts

Many full-service brokerage firms offer wrap account services, whereby all fees are combined in one package, including money management fees; security transaction fees; custody, brokerage, accounting, and trustee fees; and administration fees. These accounts are usually offered to high net worth clients with thresholds of six figures generally in the $250,000 to $500,000 range and higher. Fees range in the 125 to 200 basis point range, which simply means the percentage charged to manage the account. Wrap accounts are often hybrids of mutual funds and separately managed accounts overseen by investment managers. The investor deals directly with the broker, not the investment manager. Fees are often 2.5% to 3% and are split between the broker investment manager and the brokerage firm.

Wrap accounts deliver a discretionary packaged or managed product approach to investing while providing fee-based income for the manager, which stabilizes income and reduces the cyclical nature of the industry.

Internal Wrap Accounts
These accounts are usually offered by a dealer based on an internal model portfolio and managed by a portfolio manager plus an investment committee.

External Wrap Accounts
These accounts are offered by a broker acting as a consultant to the client to set parameters such as risk tolerance, asset allocation, and investment policies and usually meet quarterly to evaluate results.

Mutual Fund Wrap Accounts
Brokers or planners offer these accounts and they use several external fund managers to meet the investor's risk profile and asset allocation needs.

Pooled Fund Wrap Accounts

Counsellor/managers offer these accounts, which consist of a portion of a larger portfolio that is reported on a unitized basis. The minimum investment is $150,000. They were originally developed for smaller pension funds that weren't large enough to have separately managed accounts. These funds are sold without a prospectus and are available thorough the sophisticated investor rules. Management fees are generally 1% to 1.5%.

Checklist for Choosing a Mutual Fund or Wrap Account Manager

- What are the long-term goals of the investment manager?
- What investment style(s) does the manager use?
- What has been the previous track record and experience?
- What formal designations, degrees, and diplomas are held?
- How is the manager's performance measured?
- How would a decision be made to fire or replace the investment manager?
- How often will performance reports be issued?
- What are the total annual costs to manage the account?
- Will the advisor/firm issue a letter at the outset stating all costs, strategic alliances, and any potential conflicts of interest?
- Are fees contingent on investment performance or determined by industry benchmarks?

High-Profile Manager Leaves

When a high-profile manager leaves to join the competition, what should the investor do? Much depends on the managerial style the manager pursued and the commitment of the management team to continue to deliver the same style and investment philosophy you had originally chosen. Assuming the new manager(s) can deliver similar performance it is best to stay put. If you redeem the fund to follow the manager to the new fund family you will generally incur costs to switch.

Long-term Performance Suffers

How long should an investor remain loyal to a fund manager who underperforms the market averages? Most funds are evaluated quarterly. A short-term underperformance over several quarters may be due to the market style being out of favour. However, if the manager continues with poor performance for a complete market cycle, then it's time to part company. In the short-term it is possible to suffer one, two, or even a few bad quarters, but rarely would you switch managers unless the poor results continued into several bad quarters.

We live at such a hectic pace with so many things competing for our time that WRAP accounts are an ideal solution to our money management problems. As well, most of us do not have the knowledge or temperament to make our own decisions. These facts bode well for the continued growth of both WRAP accounts and mutual funds in Canada for the foreseeable future.

Specialty Non-Discretionary Fee-Based Accounts

One of the greatest growth areas for investment dealers is the move from commission-based to fee-based investing. An alternative to the discretionary management of a WRAP account or the normal commission-driven advisor account is the non-discretionary fee-based investment account, which also combines the flexibility, control, and personal advice of an advisor. These accounts usually offer a set number of transactions for which the investor pays a simple annual fee. The major benefit is the investor still has a personal investment advisor to assist in the development and implementation of personal investment strategies.

Many investors assume that fee-based advisors are the most objective, but this is not necessarily so. Honesty, integrity, trust, experience, and education are more important considerations than how the advisor is paid.

Dividend Reinvestment Plans (DRIPS)

One very low cost alternative to full-service commission rates is the dividend reinvestment and share purchase plans offered by many large Canadian companies. These plans offer investors a convenient way to increase their equity holdings by reinvesting dividends from shares without paying a brokerage commission. Some companies also offer new share purchases at a discount to market price, and some even allow

DRIP members to buy additional shares for cash with no purchase costs.

Approximately 80 publicly traded companies offer shareholders a DRIP; all have paid dividends for over 25 years and 40 of the 80 have paid dividends for over 50 years. Reinvested dividends return dividends themselves, and little dividends become big dividends when compounded.

One very convenient way to become involved in a DRIP program is to join the Canadian Shareholder's Association. Their members receive exclusive access to a range of materials to assist with building an investment portfolio.

Discount Brokerage Fees

These firms compete for your business on price. There are no frills, no advice, and no hand holding when markets are bad. Savings can amount to as much as 85% on stock transactions, dependent upon volume and price over standard commission costs at full-service brokers.

A sample of the savings on commissions available from a discount broker versus a full service broker vary widely.

Volume	Price	Full-Service Broker	Discount Broker
100 shares	$20	$75 — $85	$30 — $45
1,000 shares	$20	$300 — $450	$75 — $85

When it comes to mutual fund transactions the discounters charges are as follows:

- Front-end loads vary between 1% and 2%.
- Back-end loads will assess a deferred sales charge based on the length of time the fund is owned.
- Back-end redemptions usually start at 5% to 5.5% and decline to zero after six or seven years.
- No-load funds have no buying or selling commissions; however, often a $40 to $50 transaction fee is incurred on the purchase or sale.
- Short-term trading fees are charged by some mutual fund companies when you redeem funds within a specified period of time, generally on front-loaded funds redeemed within 90 days of purchase.

Two major advantages offered by discount brokers are 24-hour access, seven days a week, and computerized personal trading capabilities to place your own orders at even greater discounts than those placed through their order desk.

Fee-Based Administrative Account Services

Beyond the traditional fees and commissions we have discussed so far, there are often many other fees, including the following:

- **Registered Plans** — Registered Retirement Savings Plan (RRSPs), Registered Retirement Income Funds (RRIFs), Life Income Funds (LIFs), and Registered Education Savings Plans (RESPs) usually cost between $50 to $150 per account. Discount brokers would charge less than full-service brokers. Registered plans that hold only mutual funds might carry an even lower fee between $25 to $50.
- **Non-arm's length mortgage** for a principle resident usually carries a surcharge of between $150 to $300.
- **Private mortgage, investment corporation, or small business investment shares** also cost between $150 to $300 upon receipt into a registered plan.
- **Annual administration fees** for mortgages can range from $100 to $250. Other fees can apply to mortgages such as renewal fees, discharge fees, set-up fees, rate and term changes, and legal fees, which can cost several hundred dollars. With interest rates so low it would be hard to justify the costs of placing a mortgage into a registered account in today's market.
- **Certificate, custody, and registration** — safekeeping and registration in client's name cost $25 to $50 per certificate.
- **Statement search, trade investigation** vary from $25 to $50 per hour.
- **Transfer out** — full transfer is $50 to $100; partial transfer is $25 to $100.
- **Substitution or swaps** of securities range from $0 to $25.
- **Electronic transfers** are $15 to $25 per security.
- **Telephone and wire transfer** are $8 to $30 per transaction.
- **NSF charges** are $20 to $30 per cheque.
- **Stop payment request** is $20 to $30 per cheque.

Mutual Fund Fees

- **Early redemption fee** is up to 2% or more of redeemed units within 90 days.
- **Switch fees** are between 0% and 2% to switch within same fund family and are usually charged at the broker's discretion.
- **Set-up fees** are usually incurred with no-load funds as a one time charge when opening an account.
- **Systematic withdrawal fees** can be charged annually or per withdrawal.

How Much Should You Pay?

The cost of doing business with any financial professional should be based on the services performed and value-add provided by

What will it cost?

the advisor. The degree of financial knowledge the investor has acquired will also dictate the type of services required — the less knowledge the investor has the more apt will be the need for professional advice.

Obviously the investor would like the most service possible for the least cost. Afterall when you pay lower fees or commissions you have more to reinvest.

How Much Can You Save Me?

Whenever I was asked this question as a stockbroker, I would respond with a question. "Do you mean on commission costs or by keeping you out of trouble by ensuring your asset allocation strategies are appropriate for the current market cycle?" Almost always this question related to the transaction costs to which I would reply, "Never begrudge paying a professional his due." You have to spend a dollar to make a dollar.

What's in It for Me?

This question usually arises when the investor is attempting to assess the value-added services the advisor can provide. You will want to know whether transactions will be handled quickly, efficiently, and accurately; what research and information reports are available; how often statements and portfolio performance reports can be expected; and in general how you will benefit from establishing a relationship with the advisor.

Conflict of Interest

Investors want to be sure that the advisor has no bias to particular products or families of funds. Don't be afraid to ask outright whether the advisor has any personal ties or conflict of interest with any recommended investments for your portfolio.

Costs Appropriate for Service

No one should begrudge paying for services delivered as promised or portfolio performances expected as per market benchmarks. When things go wrong and services or performances don't measure up, what should the investor do? Start by letting your advisor know your concerns. You should not have to pay full commissions or fees for substandard service or advice. Most advisors would meet this request. They know you should only pay for results.

FEES AND COMMISSIONS Table 6–3

Great Debate — Which is Best?

Front-load, back-redemption, low-load, no-load, WRAP-fees, or commission per transaction?

1993

Toronto Stock Exchange 300 Index — Stocks increased	+ 32.5%
Scotia Capital Markets Universe — Bonds increased	+ 18.1%
Mutual Fund — Money market increased	+ 4.6%

The No-Help, No-Advice Investor invested in money market funds with a bank or trust. Based on excellent year-end numbers he decides to switch to equity and bond funds and redeems his money market funds.

1994

Toronto Stock Exchange 300 Index — Stocks decreased	– 0.2%
Scotia Capital Markets Universe — Bonds decreased	– 4.3%
Mutual Fund — Money market increased	+ 4.3%

The No-Help, No-Advice Investor is terribly discouraged at year-end results and realizes he would have been better off leaving everything invested in money market funds so he switches back incurring a loss by redeeming his equity and bond funds.

1995

Toronto Stock Exchange 300 Index — Stocks increased	+ 14.5%
Scotia Capital Markets Universe — Bonds increased	+ 20.7%
Mutual Fund — Money market increased	+ 6.3%

The No-Help, No-Advice Investor, after transferring billions of dollars to money market funds at the end of 1994, gets whip-sawed once again when equity and bond funds recover.

Summary:

There is no debate! Statistics show that most investors choosing **No-Help**, **No-Advice** investments do not do as well as investors who seek help and advice from an advisor.

"Adopt the pace of nature; her secret is patience."
— Emerson

Compensation Summary

A greater proportion of investors are older, more sophisticated, and better educated. As a result these savvy investors are conducting at least a portion of their trading transactions through the bank's discount broker division, and they expect commission discounts from their full-service dealers. While some investors have moved their entire portfolios to a discounter, many others prefer

65

the best of both worlds — advice from their full-service dealer and low commission costs from their discounter. This is really not fair to the full-service professionals who want to earn their business by providing lots of value-added services. Affluent clients of full-service brokers demand portfolio and asset allocation management, lots of current research and market information, and high-tech, high-touch service; and the broker should be paid for providing same.

In the final analysis only the investor can judge the value of the services provided.

"You don't get a fistful of dollars without picking up some knowledge and wisdom along the way and you should expect to pay for same."
— Graydon Watters

Part II

CHARACTERISTICS

AND TRAITS OF

FINANCIAL ADVISORS

Characteristics and Traits of Financial Advisors

One of the most popular interactive group exercises enjoyed by participants in our workshops is how to find that special person to handle your financial affairs. What characteristics and traits would you want this person to have? We have collected a wide assortment of needs, wants, and goals as expressed by seminar and workshop participants during the last five years. What stands out more than anything else is the fact that 90% of participants list their greatest concern as, "**How to find a good financial advisor?**"

Some characteristics and traits are requested more often than others and some are rarely mentioned. In virtually every program, however, trust, honesty, or integrity are listed as the first or second bullet as to importance in the selection process. In fact these three words are mentioned so often they account for over 50% importance in choosing an advisor. Often participants will make statements or ask questions pertaining to objectivity or disclosure. The following is a want list of those special characteristics and traits that prospects and clients cherish in their advisors:

Accessible	Comfortable rapport	Dedicated to servicing any
Accountable	Commitment	size client
Affordable	Communicates at my level	Dependable
Age compatibility	Community minded	Disclosure
Appearance	Compensation	Does he or she represent
Approachable	Competence	one family of funds or
Articulate	Competitive	many?
Availability for me	Comprehensive knowledge	Does not rush me
Benchmarking performance	Computer literate	Dog owner
Bi-monthly reporting	Confident	Down to earth
Bonded business and finan-	Confidentiality	Dynamic
cial credentials such as: B.	Conflict of interest	Easy-to-read statements
Comm., FCSI, CFP, RFP, CLU	Conservative	Easy to relate to
Breadth and depth of	Consistent track record	Easy to talk to
knowledge	Constant upgrade of skills	Educated
Broad-based capability	Costs appropriate for services	Empathy
(full service)	Costs within means	Empowerment
Bulletproof your investments	Counselling skills	Energy
Captive agent	Creative ability	Enthusiasm
Caring personality	Creative ideas	Ethical
Certified	Credentials	Excitement
Chemistry	Customized planning	Experienced

Explains my options clearly
Feedback
Feel safe
Financially stable personally
Firm but not aggressive
Focused goals
Follows own
   recommendations
Foresight
Formal education
Frequent review of
   financial plan
Friendly
Full disclosure
Full service
Geographically close
Global exposure (worldwide)
Global investor
Good advice
Good business connections
Good communicator
Good financial background
Good hand-holder
Good industry contacts
Good interpersonal skills
Good listener
Good personal background
Good public relations
Good qualifications
Hands-on experience
Hard worker
Has your best interests
   at heart
Have good rapport
Helpful
High self-esteem
Holistic
Honest
How compensated?
How much can he or she
   save me?
How much do you charge?

I'm the hunted
Independent
Informed, current, and
   up-to-date
Innovative
Insightful
Integrity
Interested in my goals
Investigative mind
Investment preference bias
Is the initial meeting free?
Keeps in touch
Keeps me informed
Knowledgeable
Lifelong learner
Low pressure
Makes me feel important
Master plan
Mentor
Multi-dimensional investing
Negotiable
Network of specialists
Not a friend or relative
No B.S.
No conflict of interest
No jargon
No personal ties
No pressure sale
Non-judgmental
Not a used car salesman
Not overbearing
Not too aggressive
Not too pushy
Not too slick
Nurturing
Objective
Offers modeling software
On-going relationship
On-line information systems
Opinionated
Organized
Outstanding client references

Passionate about work
Past performance
Patience
Performance motivated
Personal circumstances
Personal lifestyle
Personality compatible
   with mine
Phone access/response time
Positive attitude
Preliminary consultation
Prepares formal or verbal
   reports
Presentation
Privacy of account
Proactive versus reactive
Proven track record
Psychic
Punctual
Quarterly updates
Quick and "on the ball"
Readily available
Realistic expectations
Realistic goals
Reasonable cost
Reasonable fee/commission
   structure
References
Referrals
Reliable
Reputation
Research
Resources/capital in
   business
Respected by peers
Returns calls promptly
Risk stance
Risk tolerance
Safety of a large institution
Salaried versus commission
Savvy
Sense of humour

Sensitive

Service and results oriented

Should be objective

Similar client profiles to mine

Similar investment
 philosophy

Sincere

Small clientele

Soft sell

Sophisticated

Speaks in lay terms

Specialist network

Stable

Steadfast

Strategist

Successful personally

Supply regular newsletters

Support staff

Technical support

Temperament

Testimonial

Thorough — intense
 investigation

Timely advice

Timely recommendations

Trustworthy

Unbiased

Understands your goals

Up-to-date

Value-added

Versatile

Vision

Volunteers time to community

What has he or she done for
 me lately?

What's in it for me?

Who pays?

Will be available long-term

Will stick with plan

Wisdom

Works with your investment
 philosophy

Works with/meets with top
 fund managers

Seven

Partnerships are Built on Trust

WE HAVE BECOME CONDITIONED BY THE TIMES WE LIVE IN TO treat every salesperson as a suspect. As one participant in a recent seminar said to me, "Sometimes I feel like I am the hunted!" Therefore the first barrier that must be overcome before developing a relationship is suspicion. You must be open to developing a partnership based on the salesperson's ability to create trust and be confident in his/her professional investment management skills.

During the first meeting with a prospective investor the planner's goal is to establish credibility. And during this initial exploratory consultation and fact-finding session the planner is in the primary role of "listener." His/her job is to create a comfortable climate or support structure for you to discuss openly and honestly your needs and wants, dreams and ambitions, and goals and objectives. He or she must make sure that you have realistic expectations of portfolio profitability and overall performance. More dreams and goals are dashed because of unrealistic expectations. Therefore your planner will try to identify reasonable needs and wants, then encourage you to set goals that are attainable. With your commitment and understanding the planner will create the action steps required for a results oriented game plan.

"Fidelity is seven-tenths of business success."
— James Parton

The ultimate goal of a professional planner is to empower clients to take responsibility for their personal self-development through lifelong learning about investments and financial planning under the wing of his/her tutelage.

71

Getting to Trust

During the initial fact-finding session a good planner should ask you open-ended questions, often beginning with the **5Ws** — **Who**, **What**, **When**, **Why**, **Where**...and also **How?** This format is designed to keep you talking and the planner listening. Prior to your first meeting with a planner why not review how you would answer the following questions:

1. What are your financial dreams and goals for the future?
2. Why is financial planning important to you?
3. What are your lifestyle dreams and wants for the future?
4. Who are the most important people in your life?
5. Where would you like to live in retirement?
6. When do you expect to retire?
7. What's important about success to you?
8. What else?
9. What else?
10. And finally, How do you make important decisions?

The business of ethical persuasion begins with the planner who is a good listener; who can truly focus on your needs.

Does Corn Have Ears?

One of the most common complaints we hear is, "My advisor doesn't listen to me and doesn't seem to care." During the initial interview with an advisor be aware of who is doing the most talking. The advisor's role is to ask the appropriate questions and then listen to what you have to say to get to know you. Later, during the initial consultation, the investor should actively pursue his/her own agenda by asking questions of the advisor to determine if he or she has the right credentials to merit his/her business. The best advisors take notes during the interview to help listen and so as not to overlook any significant details in future meetings.

Relationship Marketing

Every year during the heat of RRSP season we are deluged with information from the financial service industry — banks, trusts, mutual fund, brokerage, and insurance companies. We're prospected by brokers, agents, representatives, account executives, counsellors, clerks, telemarketers, financial planners, and so on. The question most of us ask is, "Aren't these people all salespersons in one form or another and if so, how will I know my best interests are being served if I were to deal with one of them?" This question stops more people in their tracks than any other, which most often leads to procrastinating about one's financial affairs because many of us just don't know where to start or who to trust.

"A prudent question is one-half of wisdom."
— Baron

The myriad of products and financial intermediaries is overwhelming. People are becoming increasingly uninformed at an accelerating rate. Change, new companies, new product offerings, and variations of these are leading to information complexity, causing people to buy differently. Information overload, lack of accurate information, and information that is changing so fast results in the consumer making buying decisions by default. They take the line of least resistance and often deal with their local bank or trust company because these institutions are perceived to be the most trustworthy. Brokers, agents, and planners lose out because they are considered the least trustworthy.

These facts have led to an absolute bonanza for the banks and trusts during the last decade. They have been preaching relationship marketing, which is really a form of data base marketing. The goal of data base marketing is to fact find and gather every bit of information about the client so that the bank can obtain as much of the client's business as possible and promote multiple products.

Developing Trust

Finding and developing trust with a financial advisor is no easy task. Studies have shown that only about one in ten Canadians over age 50 have paid for a written financial plan and when asked to indicate their primary source of advice, 50% listed themselves. At a time when there are so many choices to make from hundreds of products, financial-planning advice is essential, and yet many investors avoid choosing a planner. Why? Because they have not been able to develop a trusting relationship. Trust is something we earn — it can't be bought! It can take years to build a reputation that embodies trust, integrity, and honesty and just a few minutes, by one wrongdoing, to tarnish and tear a reputation apart. When any two people meet, such as an investor and an advisor they both must make an effort to establish trust (see Table 7–1). Developing trust is a two-way street — it takes two to tango!

TEN TOP TIPS ON BUILDING TRUST	Table 7–1

1. **Communicate, communicate, communicate.**
2. Listen to each other, be open and honest.
3. Consider each other's best interests.
4. Identify common goals.
5. Develop clear expectations.
6. Always follow through on what you say you'll do.
7. Apologize when you're wrong.
8. Respect each other's values.
9. Be passionate about your convictions.
10. Nurture and care for each other.

Honesty and Integrity

These two words are mentioned along with trust more often than any others in our programs. Our fast-paced hectic times and instant media communications with sensational negative headlines have created a mindset whereby we are more suspectful of others, especially if the person is involved in sales. A classic case is the Bre-X scandal.

"Fool me once, shame on you; fool me twice, shame on me."
— Chinese Proverb

Bre-X will no doubt be remembered as the gold fraud of the 20th century. Just think of the damage this incident has caused — $3 billion dollars lost by thousands of investors who dumped the stock individually or through mutual funds. Bre-X was recommended by hundreds of advisors — in good faith, albeit as a higher risk. Now look at the loss of integrity caused by an unscrupulous few. We may never know what really happened or how the scam was orchestrat-

Let the buyer beware!

ed, but the ill will, mistrust, and questionable integrity of any advisor who so much as dabbled in even a few shares of Bre-X will tarnish some of their reputations for years to come. Unfortunately, many very honest financial advisors will likely be tainted by the same brush.

Honesty with Your Advisor

It is imperative that the investor convey all hopes, dreams, and goals for the future at the outset. During this interchange the advisor must decipher the investor's tolerance or comfort zone with respect to risk. Realistic expectations should be established in terms of market performance, service level of the account, reporting procedures, and type and frequency of contact, at the beginning of the relationship. It is important to set parameters on investment and asset allocation strategies, to establish portfolio review dates annually or more often if required, and to learn to communicate honestly and openly with your advisor. There is no substitute for personal integrity.

"Subtlety may deceive you; integrity never will."
— Oliver Cromwell

References and Referrals

If you had to make a decision on choosing an advisor based on one bullet only, what would it be? I would suggest that word would be referral. I built my investment career on my ability to be referred. Becoming referable is the easiest way for an advisor to obtain new clients and for an investor to find an advisor.

Our surveys indicate that the number one factor for choosing an advisor is trust, but 70% also said that referrals were critical in deciding which advisor to approach in the first place. From the investors perspective the credibility of a referral from a trusted family member, friend, or colleague is often the best way to find an advisor. Providing, of course, that their relationship has lasted for five or six years, long enough to have been through a complete market cycle together. A one-or two-year relationship may not be long enough to evaluate realistically. If, during the relationship, they have experienced only strong markets its easy to assume that the relationship with the advisor is excellent — after all you've only experienced the good times of an upward trending market, which makes everyone look like a hero. The true test for an acceptable referral would be from an investor who has survived the toughest times with an advisor.

75

What would make an advisor referable? An investor would probably offer the following top five essentials:

- trust, honesty, integrity, and loyalty
- listens and understands clients needs and goals
- experienced with good track record of past performance
- accessible and provides constant communications and education
- provides service, service, and service

Mentor My Master Plan

"The essential element in personal magnetism is a consuming sincerity — an overwhelming faith in the importance of the work one has to do."
— Bruce Barton

Fortunate are those who can claim a mentor relationship, especially when it pertains to financial planning. A mentor is an experienced and trusted advisor who has accumulated wisdom, which is shared with a deciple. I have been fortunate to have many mentors in my life and I have also had the privilege to mentor others. Some have been close personal relationships, others have been distant relationships, and some I have never met. Three of my mentors are Sir John Templeton, Warren Buffett and Peter Lynch. These men have spent a lifetime in investment and financial planning and they have laid down investment guidelines and principles that have withstood the test of time. Investors who have followed the advice of these three men would have ensured their financial success.

Friends and Relatives

Many people establish relationships with advisors based on referrals from family and friends. And that is a great place to start as long as the advisor is not a friend or family member. When I was a stockbroker I never solicited business from family members or close friends. If they approached me, I would consider the proposal only if it made sense to both parties, after a lengthy discussion regarding the pros and cons. The main reason to avoid people closest to you is that when things go wrong, as they inevitably do, it's very difficult to separate reality from the relationship risk.

Do You Have Similar Client Profiles to Mine?

Investors' profiles are rarely similar and yet they all want to feel needed; they want to know that their profile including their age, family and dependents, education, income, risk tolerance, investment knowledge, experience, needs and objectives, goals and aspirations, and the size of their account is compatible with the advisor's others clients.

When I started my investment career as a stockbroker I was in my mid-twenties with lots of formal education but no practical experience. I built a substantial practice, which required a staff of four assistants to look after my clientele. As my practice matured I became much more selective in opening new accounts based on personal compatibilities and size in order to be fair to my existing clients. Obviously it would make more sense for me to take on one new $200,000 account than 20 new $10,000 accounts. With my team of assistants, however, I was able to direct new prospects to the appropriate team member, who in reality would do the same things I would do; in other words my assistants were reading from the same script. Be sure to find out whether your advisor has an assistant(s) and ask whom you would be dealing with on a regular basis as well as in your advisor's absence.

Credibility

Most often we think credibility is based on years of service, experience, age, and so on. While these are obvious factors there are others.

- How well does the planner listen?
- Does the chemistry between you feel right?
- Do you feel in rapport?
- Was the planner well prepared for your meeting?
- Which of all of the types of financial intermediaries feels most appropriate?

Over several months we conducted a survey of workshop participants, which produced some interesting observations. As stated earlier in Part One of this book we believe the media has been responsible for shaping the financial planner image. The results of our survey show that participants rank intermediaries in the following order: financial planners, mutual fund advisors, stockbrokers, bankers, and life insurance agents.

Our survey is consistent with U.S. studies by the International Association of Financial Planners which ranked the choice of intermediaries in the same order. And finally, our studies have also shown that investors are facing information overload therefore knowledge and accurate advice is a growth business.

Credibility

Upwards of 80% of investors require financial planning advice and sales assistance.

SURVEY OF WORKSHOP PARTICIPANTS   Table 7–2

As a result of your planning you have decided to invest more aggressively to include owner-ship of stocks, equities, and or mutual funds in your portfolio. Who would you choose to make these purchases?

Financial Planner	43%	*Discount Broker*	7%
Accountant	1%	*Stockbroker*	17%
Bank or Trust Officer	9%	*Mutual Fund Advisor*	22%
Insurance Agent	1%		

Confidentiality

This is a very dangerous issue to pursue. Imagine, you have a long-term relationship with an advisor who knows everything about you and your family. Would you want your advisor to disclose your lifestyle situation to potential clients or other people? It's a counterproductive exercise at best because an advisor would only release the names of highly satisfied clients for reference so the information wouldn't be very valuable anyway.

One way to deal with this thorny issue would be to ask the advisor for the names of other professional colleagues, such as accountants, lawyers, or insurance agents, who might be familiar with his/her work. These professionals would probably know the advisor's capabilities. A little persistence and diligence by the investor will usually uncover any negatives about an advisor.

High-Pressure Sales

High-pressure selling belongs in the automobile showroom and maybe not even there. When it comes to money most people have such deep-seated fears about issues of security and an aversion to the possibility of losing some of their money that any hint of pressure by an advisor will send them scurrying for cover. Look for a firm, factual selling presentation and a softer, less aggressive sales pitch from your financial salesperson.

Non-Judgmental

Some advisors feel they need to use aggressive persuasion to convince you to comply with their wishes. In the process they could have too much to say about your character or standards and those of your loved ones. You're the best judge of how much is too much, but if you're at all uncomfortable check out the competition. In the final analysis your needs and goals are what matters most, and these should not be compromised. When a salesperson uses browbeating tactics or is judgmental about issues that you deem important, they in effect are controlling you. Most people prefer to be in a relationship that provides nurturing, genuine caring, and leaves both parties feeling energized. The lack of these three characteristics can all take away from our willingness to trust. Misused or misappropriated these traits erode trust and the investors only sensible alternative is to seek out another financial professional.

"An optimist is a person who sees a green light everywhere, while the pessimist sees only the red stoplight...The truly wise person is colourblind."
— Dr. Albert Schweitzer

Eight

Personality Compatibilities

THAT SPECIAL MAGIC THAT HAPPENS WHEN TWO PEOPLE MEET AND you know the relationship will work is the situation you are looking for with your advisor. You should be very discerning at the outset — after all you're dealing with your second most important asset — your financial health! Incidentally, the longer this meeting lasts the greater the likelihood of developing a relationship.

Good Interpersonal Skills

In all communications a person must become a fabulous listener before becoming a good communicator. We often hear in our seminars and workshops, "My broker doesn't listen to me or my advisor doesn't seem to hear or understand my needs." Investors need to know that their advisor is a real person. They want to know that their advisor cares and is prepared to listen. When an investor knows that the advisor cares, the door is open to consummate a relationship.

"They never taste who always drink; They always talk who never think."
— Matthew Prior

Investors want choice, today! They want products or services described to them and they want the ability to choose with the help of their advisor. Investors do not choose an advisor based on what is said; they choose based on what the advisor means. Many times the advisor is only helping the investor articulate what he/she already knows. The investor simply wants a relationship with a credible advisor which will be measured on the authenticity of the interpersonal communication skills between the two.

Good Rapport

The best communicators speak from their own experience. They use "I" which is much more powerful than "you." Speaking in the first person is very empowering. Advisors who utilize this skill are usually more successful at developing good rapport, at achieving personal growth, at the art of persuasion; in fact it is the language of leadership.

Core Values

Investors are looking for advisors who mirror their core values. It's human nature to value those characteristics and traits we embrace for ourselves. Those people who share similar philosophies with us often feel like our altar ego or kindred spirit, which makes it easy to develop trust. Investors want a trusting relationship with an advisor who exudes confidence above all else, and they make their choices based on instincts and gut feelings.

Speak in Lay Terms

"Common sense is very uncommon."
— Mark Twain

Many brokers, advisors, and planners speak in Bay Street jargon, which creates confusion and anxiety for the consumer. Investors want to deal with someone who speaks in lay terms, who is understandable and sensitive to their needs. A recent survey by a major financial institution showed that 50% of consumers found mutual fund investing more confusing than programming their VCR. The result is that many of them do nothing which, of course, is the worst thing they could possibly do. Advisors who are down to earth and can explain how investments work and what financial options make most sense will attract the most clients.

Caring Personality — Nurturer

Most people have a deep-seated need to be nurtured. A caring advisor helps the investor take the necessary steps to accomplish his/her objectives. Advisors know intuitively that many of their clients are frequently victims of their own circumstances and can be their own worst enemies. The advisor's job is to help keep clients on track. He or she should be skillful in the art of negotiation and have a knack for using gentle persuasion. Ideally you want an advisor who can zero in on your hot buttons to be able to reach you in your comfort zone.

Personality Similar with Mine

Most people like themselves; if they didn't they would change into someone more likable. And most people like and can easily relate to someone who is just like themselves. That is not to say that opposites don't attract; its just easier getting along with your own kind. When two people are on the same wave length they tend to energize each other. Chemistry and empathy are two of the more important characteristics to get a true measure of compatibility.

Friendly and Approachable

Some of the best planners/advisors have introvert personalities that match their analytical inquisitive nature. They're at their best when engaged in research or designing portfolio asset allocation or investment strategies. They are intelligent, quick-witted and usually attain first quartile performance. So what is wrong with this picture? More often than not this star performer hasn't developed strong personal resource skills. The question you need to ask is, "What's more important, Mr. Personality or Mr. Portfolio Performance?" Most investors would choose the latter, however they still want to deal with someone who is approachable, friendly, and has good counselling skills.

Makes Me Feel Important/Helpful

The best relationships leave both parties feeling great about themselves and each other. There are no issues of control here, rather each person energizes the other. What transpires is a spiritualistic or holistic meeting of the minds. The investor feels like the most important person in the advisor's clientele. The advisor who can make every client feel that same way is sure to succeed.

"Those whom you can make like themselves better will like you very well."
— Lord Chesterfield

Not Too Pushy, Not Too Slick

Human beings like to feel in control by their own doing as opposed to being controlled by someone else. Overly aggressive salespersons turn most people off. The ideal advisor is someone who is easy to talk to, easy to relate to, and makes you feel safe. His/her personality is positive and promotional yet not too slick. There is a fine line between being upbeat and excited about a product or service versus being too aggressive, pushy, and ramming something down someone's throat.

Presentation/Appearance

Something about how we dress makes a statement about our personality. Our appearance can exude positive thoughts like conservatism, stability, moderation, and safety, or it could create negative thoughts like unsteady, insecure, unprosperous, and risky. When it comes to dealing with money management most investors would expect an advisor to dress-up rather than dress-down. Business attire would be the normal expectation certainly in the larger metropolitan areas. An exception might be made in smaller towns or rural areas where the appropriate dress would be casual.

Positive Attitude

It is not always easy to maintain a positive attitude in today's world when we are bombarded daily with negative news from the media. Negative input often leads to negative output; we become like our associations. A bad attitude produces bad results and a good attitude produces good results. Failure breeds failure; success breeds success. It is really refreshing to meet an advisor with a positive "I can" attitude. We all want to deal with a winner, a person whose faith and belief system ensures success. As an investor, you deserve no less than an advisor who has a positive attitude.

Sense of Humour

Finance and investing is a serious subject and stock markets at the best of times can play havoc with your nerves. The last thing we need is a person who lacks a sense of humour. Even in a strong bull market the market climbs a wall of worry. The key to survival in these hectic times is to lighten up. Money is a serious subject and your ideal advisor should respect the power of money when managing your portfolio; and investors should not let money become their god, if they do it will destroy them. So the message for both advisors and clients is not to take things too seriously — after all it's only money!

Human Values — Is Your Planner a Good Listener?

Once rapport has been established with the partnership question it is the planner's role to informally interview you by asking a series of questions to determine your values. The key objective of this exercise is to elicit several of your dreams, goals, or needs for the future, rank them in importance, and then really get into possible outcomes. The ultimate goal is to build your hierarchy of values that both you and the planner are clear on, culminating in your happiness, security, satisfaction, or some other personal goal. Too many advisors monopolize the time they have with prospects often making presumptions instead of asking questions; trying to provide a solution before they understand the client's needs. Beware of the planner who does more talking than you during the initial interview — he or she is probably not a good listener. How could the planner possibly know what to advise or recommend for you if he or she does all of the talking?

"Some people never learn because they understand everything too early."
— Anonymous

Accessibility

Clients need to know their advisor will take an active interest in their account after the honeymoon is over. A common complaint we hear in our programs is, "He took my money, invested it, and then I never heard from him again!" Ideally you want to be able to access your advisor by telephone or in person when you have issues that need to be discussed. Some clients insist on face-to-face meetings — they want to see the whites of their advisor's eyes.

There are numerous other ways for advisors to stay in contact, using newsletters, regular performance reports, software, or cassette tapes to keep their clientele informed. Having a good sales and/or administrative assistant(s) also helps make accessibility to the advisor less of an issue.

Time and Availability

Time is money! How does your advisor allocate time? Does he or she use time efficiently? Do you feel you receive enough of his/her time and attention? This is one of the greatest reasons that investor/advisor relationships fail — usually when the investor feels neglected. The investor's most common refrain is, "Pay more attention to me!" Everyone has the same allotment of time each day — 1440 minutes to be exact. Are you getting your fair share of your advisor's time? Does he or she only phone on a renewal date and act as though you're best friends? Does he or she put aside time for you only on your request or is time offered freely? How does the time equation in your relationship feel? Is it enough?

Returns Calls Promptly

"This is a world of action, and not for moping and droning on."
— Charles Dickens

Next to not calling at all is the duration or response time to return your calls. In this high-tech era with voice mail, e-mail, faxes, and pagers we have come to expect instant communications. In some respects we are worse off today than we were a couple of decades ago. When I make a call, especially to a financial service company, and receive voice mail, I shudder. I expect immediate service, in fact I may want to enter an order to buy or sell a security and I certainly don't want to leave a message on voice mail!

Assuming your broker/advisor was on another call or away from his/her desk what would be an appropriate response time for you: minutes, hours, or days? Most investors would feel a sense of urgency when it comes to dealing with money-related issues. Don't be afraid to ask an advisor at your initial meeting how and when he or she responds to calls.

Nine

The Value of Experience

EVERYONE WANTS AN EXPERIENCED ADVISOR; DO YOU KNOW anyone who would request an inexperienced advisor? And how do you measure experience? Is it length of time in the business, or tenure; is the experience one gains based on practical hands-on market buys and sells; how many transactions would it take to say a person has experience; is it maturity based on age or wisdom gleaned from a lifetime of holistic encounters?

Seminar participants often suggest a knowledgeable advisor would be a requirement to manage their money. Further they suggest the advisor must have a proven track record. So let me ask you, "How would you know if the track record is good, and how would you prove it?" If a stockbroker stated he or she was capable of achieving a certain result how would you know if it was attainable and based on what evidence. Perhaps he or she could supply you with testimonials of other client experiences, presuming there were no confidentiality breaches. Many brokerage companies supply model portfolios as benchmarks to attain based on several previous years of data, but how could you be certain that this type of portfolio would have been bought and managed for you.

With experience, an advisor grows a business over the years to a point where client selection based on the asset value of the account becomes a priority. When an advisor is first starting a practice with very little experience he or she has lots of time to spend with clients no matter the size of their accounts. As the advisor hones his/her skills and becomes more articulate, he or she gathers the foresight to be much more selective in the search

"A little experience often upsets a lot of theory."
— Cadman

for new business (after all its easier to manage one account for $250,000 then 25 accounts with $10,000 each).

Good Advice/Recommendations

"A person's judgment is no better than their information."
— *P.R. Lamont*

The universe of advisors consists of tens of thousands of individuals providing advice and recommendations to clients who all desire the best in the industry. If you were to divide the advisors into four quartiles from best to worst, everyone would want to have a relationship with a first quartile manager. The top advisors/managers earn their reputation over time by accumulating a track record based on past performance. During this time they polish their counselling skills, they learn to be innovative, and with years of experience they gain insights that enable them to become very opinionated about their investment recommendations.

UNIVERSE OF INVESTMENT ADVISORS Table 9–1

1st Quartile	2nd Quartile	3rd Quartile	4th Quartile
Best	Above Average	Below Average	Worst

What's Your Downpayment?

Most clients want to deal with the most experienced seasoned professional advisor who offers maximum service for the least possible cost. In reality these two bullets just don't jibe. A new person with little experience has lots of time, whereas the established seasoned professional is looking for larger accounts. Assume you are starting off with an initial investment of $500 plus a willingness to save an additional $50 per month. How much time should you reasonably expect from a financial professional who works on a fee or commission basis? Obviously, not a lot!

Your best bet given this scenario may be to invest at the bank or trust company where you already have an account and purchase a mutual fund from their family of funds. The bank's salaried employees would be willing to give you some basic information and would spend the necessary time to get you established. As your assets build in one or more funds over the years to the $10,000 level or greater and as you gain more experience and knowledge, you might want to consider some of the higher performance mutual funds offered by the independent mutual fund companies. To access this group you will need to engage the services of a sales professional (agent, broker, planner, or advisor), if you choose a load fund; or you can deal directly with the no-load fund companies.

Specialty Marketing

We live in a very different Canada today. We are certainly a more just and tolerant society. Some of the most successful planners/advisors are capitalizing on specialty marketing themes to grow their practices, for example, ethnic brokers to ethnic clientele, or women brokers to women clientele. A good friend who was downsized with a large company was wondering what career she should pursue next. She had been a financial planning counsellor within a large corporate structure, so I suggested she continue the same career by setting up her own private practice. She took my advice and decided to specialize with women who were recently separated, divorced, or widowed, and she has built a thriving business with many referrals. Her formula for success works because she found a special niche. Here's why it works. Imagine you're a married woman who just went through a messy separation and one of its causes was money issues. Suppose further that your portion of the settlement was in the low six figures and that you had fought vigorously to win this amount. The last person you may want to talk to about money when it comes to investing is another man. Your peace of mind may be to deal with your same gender. It's easy to see why specialty marketing woman to woman has worked for this planner.

Firm but Not Aggressive

We have heard a lot of mixed opinion on this bullet in our programs. Some have stated they want to deal with an advisor who is aggressive, "a take charge type who tells me what to do." Others have wanted an agent who simply presents them with ideas who shows versatility, "who is steadfast and thorough, but not aggressive."

Most investors prefer a relationship that falls right in the middle of these two extremes: they want an advisor who is firm with the ability to communicate creative ideas in a non-aggressive manner.

No/Low Pressure Sales

As mentioned earlier most investors react negatively to the hard sell approach. Overly opinionated or pushy salespersons do not endear themselves to their clients. Given a choice most clients appreciate an advisor who is quick and on the ball, shows lots of savvy, is unbiased in his/her recommendations, has the wit of a master strategist, and can be all of these things without resorting to high pressure tactics.

How Will the Partnership Flow?

Imagine you have decided to form a partnership, then what you need to know from your advisor is, "How will you communicate with me?" Clients need to know what to expect. It is the element of surprise or the lack of follow through that upsets many client relationships. Clients need to know how their advisors choose appropriate investments for them. Even more important how do they handle problems when things go wrong. The best advisors use a three-step approach to problem solving. First they always apologize, second they fix the problem immediately, and third they look to value-add beyond fixing the problem.

Some client relationships maintain a strict business posture throughout the years; others evolve into friendships as well as the business relationship. Some planners/advisors take their clients to lunch preferring to spend time versus money; others will spend lots of money on clients, providing value-added services, including newsletters, software, computerized statements, and so on. The method your advisor uses is not as important as the fact that you are receiving value-added benefits. A good agent knows it costs ten times more to develop a new client relationship than to keep an existing one.

Realistic Expectations

Outlining realistic expectations is one of the most important roles of the financial professional. When planning for retirement the establishment of realistic goals, a plan of action to achieve them, and the action steps required to implement them must have clarity. If expectations are unreal, then even the best intended plans will fail.

Benchmarking Performance

How do you measure performance? How will you know if your advisor has done a credible job? Two essential ingredients are required to benchmark performance. First and most important is to know your comfort zone or tolerance for risk. Secondly, you develop an asset allocation strategy that matches your time frame for investing.

The next step involves measuring your performance returns in each of the major asset classes: reserves, debt, and equity against broad indices, such as 90-day treasury bills, Scotia Markets Universe Bond Index, and the Toronto Stock Exchange 300 Index. These indices provide a broad measurement of performance of their asset class, which you can use as a comparison for your portfolio. Depending upon the degree of sophistication of your investment selections, it may be necessary to benchmark your performance against subindices of these broader indices to more accurately portray your true performance.

Well Prepared/Competent

Does the advisor exude confidence? Does he or she seem well prepared? Will he or she hit the ground running? Will his/her actions speak louder than words? Is he/she a visionary with the imagination to create a plan to meet your needs?

It is essential that the person handling your money be competent. This is not always easy to assess in the first few meetings, but it will become apparent once your financial plan is put in writing. When the advisor puts your financial investment, or retirement goals, in writing, the plan must provide answers that are unique to your specific situation. It must summarize all of the relevant data into a few essential points and make concise recommendations in a few easy-to-read pages. As well, the plan should provide lots of tables, charts, and graphs as support material. You will know in your gut whether the plan makes sense and whether the advisor is competent. If you have any doubts obtain a second opinion.

Proactive versus Reactive

Most investors prefer an advisor who takes a proactive approach rather than a passive stance to money management. While performance and portfolio growth is most important to investors even more important is the advisor who provides lots of contact, attention, and nurturing. I'm absolutely amazed at how many agents take their client relationships for granted.

Make sure you choose an advisor who delivers what he or she promises; who always shows up on time and never keeps you waiting; who always finishes what he or she starts; and who treats you as the most important client.

Creative Ability

Every investor's needs and goals are different, therefore each financial or investment plan must be customized to the individual investor. The advisor must demonstrate technical knowledge, judgment, creative talent, and objectivity in dealing with the special needs and challenges presented by each potential client.

Work Ethic

The time-honoured work ethic is a trait that most investors value in an advisor. Most investors expect their advisor to work as hard or harder than themselves. Hard work is viewed as a key to success and is valued more than seat-of-the-pants street smarts or ruthlessness.

Successful

"It's not what you earn, but what you save that makes your neighbour rant and rave."
— Anonymous

Nothing breeds success like success. It is a comforting feeling to be around successful people. When it comes to managing money most investors want to deal with an advisor who has enjoyed personal financial success. If the advisor is not financially stable there is always the risk that some transactions are created to generate commission.

Personal circumstances tell a lot about an advisor: where he or she lives; what kind of car he or she drives; how he or she dresses; what clubs and associations he or she belongs to; whether he or she is community minded and engaged in volunteer activities; whether he or she is family oriented; his or her values, and as one lady in our seminar said, "Does he own a dog?"

$$10 \quad Ten$$

Compliance and Investor Protection

THE DAWNING OF THE INFORMATION AGE IS UPON US. COMPUTERS and the microchip have changed the world forever. The pace of change and new knowledge is accelerating on an exponential curve. Tremendous advances in technology and telecommunications force each of us to upgrade our skills constantly or risk being lost in the hectic interchange happening around us. The main forces driving the universal economies of the world today are business and finance. It is imperative that employees in the financial services industry commit to lifelong learning and constant upgrading of skills in order to merit your business.

Computer literacy is essential in the financial services industry. There are so many good software programs that can assist with crunching "what if" scenarios in the development of a financial plan. Planners/advisors need to stay up-to-date with the latest new offerings to remain competitive.

Education or Training

With age comes wisdom. It is a truism today that most investors have expectations to deal with the most experienced advisor and to pay the least amount possible for his/her services. Obviously this is unrealistic. A novice advisor would have lots of time to service clients but would not have the benefit of years of theoretical and practical experience. A seasoned successful profes-

"Chance favours the prepared mind."
— Louis Pasteur

"The virtuoso was once an amateur."
— Emerson

sional who has the wisdom of years has lots of knowledge and usually looks for larger accounts to maximize very limited time.

Should the goal of a financial planner be to educate or train his/her client? To educate is to teach why and wherefore; to train is to show what to do. Let me ask you a question, "Which would you rather your teenager get — sex education or sex training?" Without question, education is the greatest value a financial professional can bestow on clients.

Education versus Hands-On Practical Experience

During 1992 when we launched **Financial Knowledge Inc.**, we called on several school boards to introduce our educational programs and specifically *Financial Pursuit* a book written in 1988 which continues to enjoy tremendous sales volume success each year. Many seminar participants, including teachers, who have attended our spousal programs in corporate Canada have told me, "You've got to get this book and your programs into the school system." Eventually, our negotiations made it to the board of directors level of one of the major school boards at which point I was asked what my credentials were. I replied, "I have a Bachelor of Commerce (B. Comm.); Fellow of Canadian Securities Institute (FCSI); and I am a Certified Financial Planner (CFP) with 10 years' banking and 23 years' investment advisory experience. They absolutely floored me with the next question. "No, Mr. Watters you don't seem to understand. We want to know what your doctorate is in?" That just about says it all. What they were looking for was a person with theoretical knowledge — a Ph.D. in plumbing, heating, and drains; pool, hearts and dice; or perhaps a posthole digger. Whereas I was offering three recognizable degrees and designations in the financial service industry, but more importantly, 33 years of practical hands-on experience. And a little experience in the stock market is much more valuable than a lot of theory.

During my tenure on Bay Street, I learned about client relationships and expectations and their investment psychology; how to retain clients with effective holistic partnership strategies; and about life cycle marketing where you practice fitting products, price, and service to client needs. I also learned that if you hold the right investments, but at the wrong time of a market correction such as October 1987, there is nothing you can do after the fact except provide crisis communications. This is the time when an advisor can provide the greatest value, transforming negative client energy into a positive market experience.

Reputation and Respect

Reputations are earned; they are not a given. It is difficult to hide from a bad reputation. A reputation always precedes its owner. Investors should determine the character of the advisor they plan to work with. A little due diligence at the outset of the relationship could save you a lot of grief later.

Don't hesitate to talk to colleagues and peers of any advisor you're considering. Does the advisor maintain relationships with his/her peers and is he or she held in high esteem by them? Has the advisor achieved any rewards and/or industry recognition?

Proven Track Record

Seminar/workshop participants often select track record as an important consideration when choosing an advisor. How would you document this claim? Most times you have to rely on the advisor's word and/or some historical portfolio models. Perhaps the advisor might give you a few client names to call with their permission, but how valuable would that be? He or she is certainly not going to send you to someone who would rate him/her poorly.

"Well done is better than well said."
— Benjamin Franklin

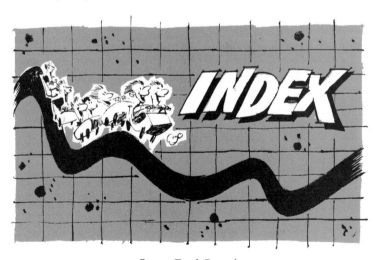

Proven Track Record

95

One of the interesting features with mutual fund investing is that all funds "hang out their laundry" for all to see. At any time you can view the track record of a mutual fund for daily, weekly, monthly, and one-, three-, five-, to ten-year performance figures, which enables the investor to document exactly what results the fund has achieved historically. The only question now is, "Would the advisor have had you invested in the better performing funds?"

How to Appreciate Your Advisor

Most experienced investors know that it takes a good client as well as a good advisor to achieve profitable investment results. They also know that the advisor will be wrong a certain percentage of the time. To achieve optimum results on your invested capital the following traits will endear you to your advisor:

- Clients should understand that they are equally responsible with their advisor in the selection process of securities — this is an advisory and not a managed money relationship.
- Clients know that there are only three decisions they must make: what to buy, when to buy, and when to sell, and they are not going to be right all the time.
- Establish at the outset of your relationship how often you should be in contact, who should initiate the call, for how long, and what time of day is best to call.
- Place all operational or administration requests verbally by phone as well as in writing to make it easy for the advisor or his/her assistant to handle your request.
- The greatest way to say thanks to your advisor is to send referrals which is the lifeblood of the industry.
- The next best way of saying thanks is to buy a gift, send flowers, or take your advisor to lunch.

Demonstrates Sincerity

Canadians are very self-conscious when it comes to talking about money. They need to know that the advisor thinks that their money is the most important in the world because to them it is. The advisor must talk about their money free of any pretense or deceit. Most investors are able to tell if false claims or baseless assertions are being made. Unfortunately, the unscrupulous are able to entice new victims everyday and some folks, especially the elderly, are easy prey for the ruthless.

Bonded/Errors and Omission Insurance

At a very early stage in the interview the investor should ascertain that the advisor is bonded and insured if he or she works for a company and/or carries errors and omission insurance if he or she is a sole practitioner. We live in an extremely litigious society and timing mistakes and market cycles are a fact of life. Sometimes in this complicated and unpredictable world, no matter how skilled or experienced the advisor, investments can sour and disputes can arise as to fault. Just knowing there is insurance coverage in place can alleviate anxiety for both parties.

Ethics Committee

Every financial planning professional has an obligation to maintain high standards of fundamental and technical competance, morality, and integrity. Each of the professional organizations mentioned in Chapter 5 has an ethics committee. It is a requirement before being considered for licensing or a designation to report any legal or disciplinary proceedings by any government or licensing, professional, or self-governing body. Full details of any and all infractions, violations, or lawsuits must be reported in a timely fashion. These measures are in place to serve the public and business community so that they can rely on the professional for sound advice.

The integration of the four pillars of financial institutions has encouraged the multiple licensing of products so much so that it is no longer clear to the layperson what primary business their financial institution is in. As well, the regulatory process has not been able to keep pace. Presently there are several organizations attempting to provide self-regulatory organization (SRO) for their members.

Investment Dealers Association (IDA) — for salespeople of member firms

Investment Funds Institute of Canada (IFIC) — for mutual fund salespeople

Financial Planners Standards Council of Canada (FPSCC) —
for salespeople who earn the Certified Financial Planner (CFP)
designation

The goal of the Ontario Securities Commission is to have one
single SRO for all securities salespeople in place by March 1, 1998.

Full Disclosure

The question every investor must ask is, "Is the advisor disclosing
all of the information necessary in order to make an informed
decision?" Complete, full, plain, and true disclosure is your right
as an investor. Many investors do not take the time to probe
deeply enough, nor do their advisors always offer enough information to make the best decisions.

"The mind is like the stomach. It is not how much you put into it that counts, but how much it digests."
— A.J. Nock

The responsibility for disclosure is three-fold:

1. the advisor
2. the company
3. the investor

Every company that issues a new security and every mutual
fund company prepares reports and prospectuses. When an
investor purchases a mutual fund a prospectus is mailed with the
conformation of the transaction. It is important for the investor to
read and understand the investment being acquired. Most
investors do not take the time to read a prospectus, relying on
their advisor to make decisions for them — then when an investment turns sour they blame the advisor. A prospectus can be very
intimidating for some people, however, it can offer valuable
insights into the company. The company's prospectus is designed
to disclose all of the intricate details of the underlying investment,
such as the following:

- An overview of the company, including its growth and business strategy, past performance, industry overview, competition, sales and marketing strategies
- Eligibility for investment under prudent investment standards
  of the various Insurance Companies Act, Trust and Loan
  Companies Act, Financial Institutions Act, Pension Benefits
  Standards Act for Canada, and the Pensions Benefits Act for
  various provinces, include
  - regulatory requirements
  - selected financial information

- management's discussion and analysis of financial condition and results of operations
- executive compensation salary, stock options, and incentive programs
- use of proceeds and plan of distribution
- description of share capital
- dividend policy
- principal and selling shareholders and escrow arrangements
- dilution
- risk factors
- promoter
- auditors, registrar, and transfer agent
- legal matters
- material contracts
- purchaser's statutory rights
- financial statements
- certificate of the promoter, the company, and the underwriter

Typical Disclosures in a Mutual Fund Simplified Prospectus

- Summary of funds expenses, detailing the management fees charged to the Funds and the management expense ratio, and operating expenses
- Summary of investor expenses, detailing sales charge option, redemption charge option, exchange option, transfer fee, redemption fee, registered plan fee (trustee), and replacement certificates
- Summary of dealer compensation, detailing sales charge or commission paid to dealer, service or trailer fees, other sales incentives
- Summary of the Funds and description of the units offered
- Management of the Funds
- Management fees and operating expenses
- Investment strategies, objectives, and practices
- Risk factors
- Dealer compensation
- Investor services — retirement plans and registered accounts (RRSP, RRIF, RESP, GRSP, DPSP), PAC plans, systematic withdrawal plans, transfer privileges, redemption of units, dividends or distributions, and minimum account balances

- Income tax considerations
- Auditors, transfer agent, registrar, and custodian
- Purchasers statutory rights

Prospectuses must meet regulatory approval as to their content and wording. Overviews of the company or mutual fund are contained in a summary format at the front of the document with a table of contents that provides the investor with the ability to access any relevant material of interest. As you can see there are substantial details provided for the investor in a prospectus. **Use it to your advantage!**

What Is a Broker's Liability to a Client?

The relationship between broker and client is one of agent and principal. At least three types of duty may arise from this:

1. Contact of agency
2. Duty of care
3. Fiduciary duty

Contract of Agency

- To abide by the terms of any agreement which places duties on the broker
- To do such things as necessary to achieve the obvious intent of the broker/client agreement

Duty of Care

- To use reasonable care and skill in advising or effecting any transactions
- To handle the client's affairs to the standard of proficiency that can be expected from a responsible broker
- To carry out the client's instructions in accordance with standard industry practice
- To ensure that any information is accurate and that any advice given is reasonable and appropriate

Fiduciary Duty

The existence or extent of fiduciary duty depends on a number of factors, including the following:

- The degree of control the broker exercises over the client's account
- The role of the broker, investment advisor, or simple order taker
- The nature of the trade or trades in question
- The age, education, intelligence, investment sophistication, or knowledge of the client
- The degree of reliance the client places on the broker

In general, as a fiduciary, the broker must

- act honestly and in good faith
- ensure that no personal interest conflicts with the client's interests
- fully disclose all material facts and any conflict of interest or potential conflict of interest

Duty of Care

- explain the prudence of particular transactions and/or the consequences of trading patterns including a discussion of broker commissions and client profits or losses

How to Agitate Your Advisor

Sometimes the shoe is on the other foot whereby the advisor should question how to choose a good client. Most clients are reasonable and courteous people; however some can be really toxic and cause more anxiety than they are worth. Nothing the advisor does can please this client who will question every recommendation, second guess every decision, complain about costs, and generally harass the advisor and his/her staff. Advisors should avoid clients who

"There are some clients who would make a cup of coffee nervous."
— Graydon Watters

- demand more of the advisor's time than the size of the account warrants
- have totally unreasonable profit expectations
- demand unreasonable deep discounts
- window shop and never open an account

- are not totally open and honest
- second guess all of the advisor's recommendations

Canadian Investor Relations Institute (CIRI)

The CIRI was formed a decade ago as a professional organization to provide communication between its members and public corporations, investors, and financial communities. The mission of the CIRI is accomplished by providing strong investor relations programs to help companies maximize share value, reduce the cost of capital, and address the challenges of changing markets, and shareholder needs.

Communication is fundamental to shareholder confidence, and the Investor Relation (IR) specialist must always ensure that disclosure is full, plain, and true. A stock promoter, on the other hand, does not always practice disclosure and often gets caught up in promotional type activity, which can at times be misleading. It is important for the investing public to understand the difference between investor relations that comply fully with securities legislation that is supported by the Toronto Stock Exchange versus promotional activity that would not meet the standards of securities legislation and yet may still be approved by other exchanges, such as the Vancouver Stock Exchange which have less stringent standards.

Companies recognize the need for credible and strategic IR programs and the CIRI is doing its best to fill the need. The message for the investor is **"know your information sources!"** Differentiate between IR which supports full disclosure and stock promotion which could be misleading. In most cases, **if it sounds too good to be true it probably is!!!**

Canadian Deposit Insurance Corporation (CDIC)

The Canadian Deposit Insurance Corporation (CDIC) is a government agency that insures bank, trust, and loan company deposits such as chequing accounts, savings accounts, term deposits, guaranteed investment certificates (not exceeding five years), money orders, drafts, and traveller's cheques. Coverage is guaranteed and limited to a maximum of $60,000 per person, per institution, but applies to RRSPs, RRIFs, and non-RRSPs separately. You should always ensure, when applicable, that the issuing institution is a member of the CDIC.

Table10–1 shows an example of CDIC protection that you and another person may have with the same member institution.

CDIC PROTECTION LIMITS	Table 10–1
You	
Savings, chequing, and term deposits	$60,000
Deposits made in trust for another person	60,000
RRSPs	60,000
RRIFs	60,000
	$240,000
Spouse/Partner	
Savings, chequing, and term deposits	$60,000
Deposits made in trust for another person	60,000
RRSPs	60,000
RRIFs	60,000
	$240,000
Both of You	
Savings, chequing, and term deposits	$60,000
Total	**$540,000**

Credit Unions Central of Canada

Credit unions provide deposit and RRSP insurance for members and are regulated provincially. Coverage varies from province to province but most often is $60,000 maximum similar to banks, trust, and loan companies. The Credit Union Central of Canada oversees all credit unions with the exception of those in Québec which are regulated by the Québec Deposit Insurance Board.

Canadian Life and Health Insurance Compensation Corporation (Comp Corp)

This is the life insurance industry equivalent of the CDIC protection for bank, trust, and loan companies. The following policies qualify for protection under Comp Corp:

Class A includes life insurance policies, accumulation annuities, RRSPs, RRIFs, and any other policies that provide life insurance protection up to $200,000; and $60,000 in cash withdrawal for policies registered under the income tax act such as RRSPs, RRIFs, LIFs, and pension policies

Class B includes fixed-term annuities and disability income policies with regular payments to a maximum of $2,000 per month

Class C includes health care and dental benefits to a maximum of $60,000 per person covered plus each dependent separately

Canadian Investor Protection Fund (CIPF)

The Canadian Investor Protection Fund (CIPF) is a trust sponsored by the four Canadian stock exchanges (Vancouver, Alberta, Toronto, and Montreal) and the Investment Dealers' Association of Canada. The Fund protects the financial assets of customers in the event that a member firm becomes insolvent. In this sense, it is not unlike the Canada Deposit Insurance Corporation (CDIC) coverage for individual bank accounts.

The Canadian Investor Protection Fund covers a customer's general accounts, as well as a customer's separate accounts — RRSP, RRIF, joint account, trust, partnerships, and so on. The limit of coverage for the aggregate of a customer's general accounts is a maximum of $500,000. (Separate accounts are not combined with other separate accounts unless they are held by a customer in the same capacity or in the same circumstances.) Members of the five sponsoring bodies must provide a CIPF brochure and a copy of its policy statements to customers on request.

Protection for the Mutual Fund Investor

While no broad-based protection exists, assets are not held by the mutual fund company, rather they are held by a custodian. If the custodian firm collapses, assets are still safe because they are segregated from the custodian's assets.

The Investment Funds Institute of Canada (IFIC) states that a mutual fund's assets belong to the fund and its investors, not to the trustee who is responsible for administrative decisions, nor the manager, who is responsible for investment decisions. The following safeguards as adapted from National Policy 39 by provincial securities administration require:

• Assets of the mutual fund must be held by a trustee (normally a Canadian bank or trust company) and, therefore, are protected under banking and trust laws.

- Funds received from clients must be segregated from the dealer and sent to the mutual fund company promptly.
- The mutual fund assets must be held separate and apart from any other assets that belong to the fund's manager, custodian, or trustee.
- The mutual fund manager is prohibited by law from using the fund assets in any way other than making investments for the benefit of the unit holders.
- Regular audits (annually) by independent accountants and internal control systems to ensure conformity to industry regulations are the norm.
- Contingency funds have been set up in several provinces, including Ontario, Québec, British Columbia, and Nova Scotia, to protect investors from dishonest employees, theft, or fraud. These funds have never been drawn on since inception in the 1960s.
- Independent mutual fund dealers and institutions that sell mutual funds must post bonds as insurance against the loss of assets.
- Employees are bonded with substantial insurance coverage by their companies.

When Expectations Are Not Fulfilled

Client relationships occasionally falter for many different reasons. It is always in the best interest of the client and the broker/agent/advisor he or she deals with to resolve any dispute as quickly as possible. The worst thing either party can do is to let the issue fester and become an even larger problem by neglecting to deal with the dispute. What safeguards are available to the investor if a problem should arise? Start at Step 1 and if unresolved move to the next step.

Step 1 Lodge a complaint with your broker.

Step 2 Complain to the branch manager.

Step 3 Report your dispute to the compliance officer for the company.

Step 4 Lodge your dispute with the Investment Dealers Association (IDA). Most reputable investment companies belong to the IDA.

Step 5 For disputes involving less than $50,000 attempt to arbitrate with an impartial arbitrator as appointed by, but totally independent from, the Investment Dealers Association (IDA).

Step 6 In the event that a stock exchange bylaw has been breached and your investment firm is an IDA member your dispute could be resolved by the exchange.

Step 7 Report your case to the provincial securities commission. The IDA and the various securities commissions can regulate your dispute as to any wrong doing but they cannot award financial compensation.

Step 8 Engage the services of a litigation lawyer to investigate an unsettled financial dispute.

Eleven

In Service We Bond

ONE OF THE GREATEST COMPLAINTS WE HEAR IN OUR WORKSHOPS IS, "My advisor never calls me." It's fair to say that most of us like to be called occasionally, and sometimes the only agenda for the call should be personal rather than sales related. In a perfect world we would be dealing with an advisor who just calls to say things like: "hello, how ya doin?," "thanks for being my client," "thanks for dropping by," "thanks for the referral," and most importantly an advisor who says thank you more often.

During the 1970s and 1980s people dealt with an advisor for two reasons:

1. They provided products or services the investor wanted.
2. The investor trusted and liked the advisor.

During the 1990s the focus is on value-added services and the costs of transacting business. And trust is still as important today as it was yesterday.

When investors feel there are no value-added benefits for staying in the relationship with their advisor they will take their business elsewhere. One out of ten clients will let the advisor know they are dissatisfied; nine out of ten will simply walk away with no previous warning. But rest assured, they will spread the word!

So how do the most successful advisors provide client service? They often provide client service specialty teams, which, when structured properly, will enhance operational and administrative efficiencies, provide new referrals, increase assets under management, and provide client loyalty by focusing on individual customer value — clients are not just another number.

CLIENT SUPPORT/SERVICE LOOP　　　　　　　　　　　　Chart 11–1

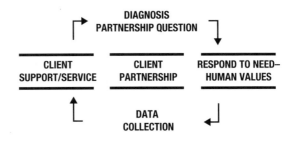

The financial service industry is not about products; it's about building successful client partnerships. Good advisors know they are in the self-improvement business — making peoples' lives better. With every new prospect I met I always asked for the opportunity to earn the client's business by providing value-added services. I understood how valuable time was for many potential clients; in fact for some clients time was more valuable than money. Consequently, I often visited clients at home during the evening or on weekends away from business hours.

Results Oriented/Outcomes

The best advisors take a no-nonsense, results-oriented approach to doing business with clients, not just on portfolio performance but also on servicing the account. They know that lack of service will eventually lead to the loss of the account. Therefore at the outset of every new relationship they establish the expectations of the client and design a game plan to deliver a specific outcome called "keeping and maintaining client partnerships." How do they meet this outcome? They use a variety of techniques that we call a service quotient.

Service Quotient

What degrees of service does your advisor provide? A good advisor worth his/her salt should be offering several of the following services:

• Keeps in touch often and has a genuine interest in my affairs.

- Stays informed, current, and up-to-date.
- Provides enthusiastic ideas and recommendations.
- Keeps me informed — provides a regular personal newsletter.
- Clips and mails articles and other items of interest.
- Sends handwritten birthday and anniversary cards, and other personal thank-you notes.
- Provides educational tools and client appreciation events.
- Has a referral network of professionals at your disposal.
- Does a competent and professional job with honesty and integrity.
- Delivers reliable, dependable service at all times.
- Provides timely and good execution on transactions.
- Issues readable account statements.
- Provides frequent reviews of financial plans.
- Offers high-tech, high-touch technology.

Informed, Current, and Up-To-Date

Interactive on-line global information systems via cable or satellite has arrived. These tremendous advances in technology and telecommunications are driving the service-based financial industry. Lifelong learning is the order of the day. Brokers and advisors must keep up-to-date to remain competitive. It is essential to provide research capabilities either in-house or through a correspondent network — clients demand this educational edge.

Keeps in Touch

Regular client contact is at the core of client service. Contact should be highly personalized as often as possible. However, diversity through the use of newsletters, articles, client appreciation events, and other educational endeavours is also greatly appreciated. Clients like to feel they are in your inner circle — a quick call from time to time just to say hello will solidify the relationship.

Newsletters or Personal Notes

Bi-monthly or quarterly personalized communication via a newsletter is a value-added service which our surveys show is greatly appreciated. I wrote a quarterly newsletter for the last eight years that I was a broker and it generated a constant stream of client contact and conversation from the articles, ideas, and recommendations I included. Many companies provide a standard newsletter that each advisor can personalize with a picture and a few comments. I would frequently clip an article to send to clients on an investment they owned, or on one I felt they should own, or perhaps a general interest article on the economy or the business cycle with a short note written on a personalized note pad. Be sure to ask if the agent you are considering provides a regular newsletter or personalized notes for clients.

Reliable/Dependable

Actions speak louder than words. Many advisors talk a great talk but are not reliable. They give the impression they are focused on doing or completing a task but then do not deliver. They make promises to do something and then are not dependable. Sometimes its because they are too busy with too much on their plate, other times it is because they have too many clients and/or are understaffed. Whatever the reason if your needs are not being met then it's time to seek out another advisor.

Some seminar participants have told us that after two or three bad experiences with advisors they just gave up in despair and managed their investments on their own.

Timely and Good Execution

When you enter a transaction to buy or sell securities, you expect the trade to be completed at a good price that reflects the current market conditions, in a timely and orderly manner. Some brokerage houses are better than others and pride themselves on this expertise. Mutual fund investors needn't worry as much because pricing is set daily at the close of the market, and the unit value to buy or sell is established based on the net asset value of all of the assets of the fund each day.

Once a trade is completed most investors like to know the details of the transaction, such as how many units were bought or sold and at what price. Some advisors report completed transactions, others don't; but most will if asked. If feedback is important to you then insist on receiving reports on your completed trades.

Confusing Account Statement

One of the greatest irritants for investors is a confusing account statement. The statement is one of the most important communication tools between the broker and the client, yet many firms still issue reports that are difficult to read. Savvy advisors supplement their firm's statements by issuing their own reports and newsletters as a valued-added service for their clients. Those brokers and firms that issue customized quarterly reports with performance returns, capital gains and losses, accrued interest and dividends, all in a user friendly format, will be rewarded with appreciative clients over the longer term.

"The financial service industry has a great record of shooting itself in the foot."
— Graydon Watters

Frequent Review of Your Financial Plan

The management of your money is a serious responsibility — yours and your advisor's. To know how well you are doing it is imperative that you establish a frequent reporting system. These reports may be verbal or written or both during the year. However, a more formalized written report should be offered at least once per year. Some advisors include modeling software as part of their review and will help their clients crunch a number of "what if" scenarios. Uppermost in the client's mind is that the broker shows he or she cares by providing regular contact, and the client wants to know when there has been a change to the game plan. As well, whenever we begin a new relationship we would like to think that it has the possibility of surviving long term — very few people are looking for "here today, gone tomorrow" relationships.

Client Appreciation Events

These events can be one of the best relationship building tools to develop loyalty and client referrals. They can range from sporting venues, arts and entertainment, and education to professional motivational speakers. I have the pleasure of delivering many client appreciation seminars each year. I find it interesting that the advisors who sponsor these events are usually always top quartile performers. They believe in spending a dollar to make a dollar; that saying thank you to their clients will lead to referrals and more new business, and they are always right.

111

21st Century Model Advisors

What characteristics and traits distinguish the best advisors from the rest of the pack? What is it that they do that ensures their success from year to year? We believe it is built around a concept we call the **5Es — energy, excitement, enthusiasm, empathy**, and **empowerment!** In the pursuit of adding value-added service for their clients the top quartile advisors use the 5Es on a continuous bases to maintain healthy client partnerships.

During your initial interview with an advisor you should be looking for these telltale signs that will let you know if there is the basis for a relationship with this person.

Energy — How much energy does the advisor exert? Is his/her energy level compatible with yours? Most people tend not to believe people with low energy. Does the advisor make eye contact, use body language, and have a physical aura that matches your chemistry?

Excitement — Does the advisor exude excitement while using firm, but gentle, persuasion and attempt to seek common ground to reach your comfort zone? Most investors want a person who uses ethical persuasion to help solve their problems.

Enthusiasm — Seminar and workshop participants tell us they want to deal with an advisor who sells peace of mind; who does not try to sell a track record; who knows how to build trust by underselling versus overselling; who knows how to discipline the mind, while encouraging the heart; who will market what they are interested in and lead them to take action. They want to deal with an advisor who is passionate about the products he or she sells and provides genuine enthusiasm for a transaction.

"If you're not fired with enthusiasm, you'll be fired with enthusiasm!"
— Vince Lombardi

Empathy — Clients want to know how the advisor feels and they need to know that he or she cares. The best advisors sell based on needs — they provide a needs analysis to understand the emotional objectives of their clients; they seek out clients fears and concerns and convey a sense of understanding and compassion in the process. As well the best advisors are charmed listeners who will offer help and support with patience. Too many advisors just play hit and run showing a total lack of concern for the clients real emotional needs. Worst still, when it comes time to invest the advisor is off and running with his/her agenda instead of focusing on the client's agenda. At the first sign of this type of lack of consideration or insensitivity the investor should begin the search for a new advisor relationship.

Empowerment — The ultimate goal for all advisors should be to empower their clients to take control of their financial futures. They teach clients to trust their instincts while providing access to the tools they'll need to succeed. By demonstrating the courage of their convictions they enable their clients to have the courage to allocate money to the various asset classes with confidence. And when clients learn to take charge of their money and to model success strategies they gain greater self-esteem.

"If you will please people, you must please them in their own way."
— Lord Chesterfield

Does your advisor embrace the 5Es?

Advisors who provide the foregoing 5Es in the pursuit of their practices are inevitably the most successful. They do one other thing — they provide continuous education knowing full well that an educated client is a client for life.

Chart 11–2 depicts the 21st Century Model Advisor. In the pursuit of value-added service the advisor tries to make $1 + 1 = 3$. They are stewards to their clients, and at all times in the pursuit of enhancing performance they exercise responsibility and are accountable.

21ST CENTURY MODEL ADVISOR Chart 11–2

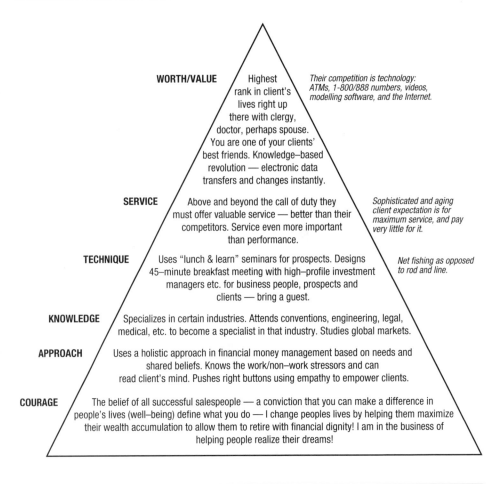

WORTH/VALUE Highest rank in client's lives right up there with clergy, doctor, perhaps spouse. You are one of your clients' best friends. Knowledge–based revolution — electronic data transfers and changes instantly.

Their competition is technology: ATMs, 1-800/888 numbers, videos, modelling software, and the Internet.

SERVICE Above and beyond the call of duty they must offer valuable service — better than their competitors. Service even more important than performance.

Sophisticated and aging client expectation is for maximum service, and pay very little for it.

TECHNIQUE Uses "lunch & learn" seminars for prospects. Designs 45–minute breakfast meeting with high–profile investment managers etc. for business people, prospects and clients — bring a guest.

Net fishing as opposed to rod and line.

KNOWLEDGE Specializes in certain industries. Attends conventions, engineering, legal, medical, etc. to become a specialist in that industry. Studies global markets.

APPROACH Uses a holistic approach in financial money management based on needs and shared beliefs. Knows the work/non–work stressors and can read client's mind. Pushes right buttons using empathy to empower clients.

COURAGE The belief of all successful salespeople — a conviction that you can make a difference in people's lives (well–being) define what you do — I change peoples lives by helping them maximize their wealth accumulation to allow them to retire with financial dignity! I am in the business of helping people realize their dreams!

Why Financial Advisors Lose Clients

We have discussed at length how to find that special person to form a partnership with, yet over time many of these relationships do not survive. Most often we assume the fall out in the relationship is due to poor market performance. Nothing could be further from the truth. While lack of performance can be one of the factors, we have compiled a list of factors from our seminars that may surprise some of you.

Is your advisor on duty or on safari?

The number one reason clients leave is lack of contact. We hear this refrain over and over again, "My advisor never calls me!" The second greatest reason that clients leave is poor service and a perceived lack of interest on the part of the advisor. The third most quoted reason is quite simply there is no value-added to the relationship, which suggests the investor is paying for no service. Here are a number of other reasons that clients give for leaving advisors:

- The advisor did not understand the client's expectations. Undersell versus oversell!
- The advisor was not conservative enough in the client's opinion.
- Tax advantaged investments often lead to trouble.
- Advisor not readily accessible, did not return calls promptly.

- Advisor was not competent, lacked knowledge.
- Advisor lacks creativity and expertise.
- Advisor did not listen to me to hear my needs and concerns.
- Advisor did not explain my options clearly in lay terms.
- Advisor did not have empathy for my goals.
- Advisor's personality was not compatible with mine.

Part III

GUIDELINES FOR

CHOOSING A

FINANCIAL ADVISOR

Twelve

Creating Your Action Plan

IN PART ONE WE CONCENTRATED ON THE IMPORTANCE OF financial planning and the various types of financial intermediaries and how they are compensated. In Part Two we explored in depth the characteristics and traits we would like a planner/advisor to have and how to select this special person. In Part Three it's time to get serious about the mechanics; none of the foregoing will have value for you unless you take action. The most important first step to creating your action plan is to know who you are with respect to risk. One of the most popular knowledge tools in our programs is a prework exercise *Investment Personality Questionnaire,* which enables participants to discover their personal investment profile and their comfort zone with respect to risk. Take a moment now to answer the questions in Worksheet 12–1 then score your results to find out your investment personality.

What is your investment personality?

119

INVESTMENT PERSONALITY QUESTIONNAIRE Worksheet 12–1

INSTRUCTIONS: Statements 1 to 16 should be answered on the basis of how strongly you agree or disagree with each statement. Questions 17 to 25 measure risk tolerance based on which statements you choose.

	Strongly Agree			Strongly Disagree	
	A	B	C	D	E
1. I want a guarantee of the income from my investments, even if I have to accept a lower yield.	☐	☐	☐	☐	☐
2. I can't afford any possible loss of capital regardless of the potential return.	☐	☐	☐	☐	☐
3. I want to be sure that I can sell my investments on short notice if necessary.	☐	☐	☐	☐	☐
4. I can't afford any significant loss of capital, but I want the best return I can get.	☐	☐	☐	☐	☐
5. I want to be sure I can get my money out of the market in case of recession or a stock market crash, even if I have to settle for a lower yield.	☐	☐	☐	☐	☐
6. I am satisfied with my yield from TDs, GICs, CSBs, CTBs, and bonds, so I would rather not invest in the volatile stock market.	☐	☐	☐	☐	☐
7. I don't feel capable of making investment decisions regarding common and preferred shares.	☐	☐	☐	☐	☐
8. I am concerned that my present savings structure will not provide the necessary income to offset the long-term effects of inflation.	☐	☐	☐	☐	☐
9. I require maximum income from my investments now and I'm not as concerned about the future.	☐	☐	☐	☐	☐
10. I have lots of income now so I want my investments to produce maximum income and growth for my retirement years.	☐	☐	☐	☐	☐
11. I want maximum capital growth potential for my retirement.	☐	☐	☐	☐	☐
12. I want a blend of safety, income, and growth right now and for my retirement years.	☐	☐	☐	☐	☐
13. I want the potential for capital growth, but I don't want to put all my eggs in one basket.	☐	☐	☐	☐	☐
14. Aggressive investors can earn higher returns and I am willing to accept the risk involved for those higher returns.	☐	☐	☐	☐	☐
15. My greatest concerns are inflation and taxes, therefore, I am willing to invest for maximum protection from these arch enemies.	☐	☐	☐	☐	☐

	A	B	C	D	E
16. I am prepared to learn as much as I can about investments through financial books and publications and investment courses, so that I can make my own investment decisions and/or use professional help to attain my goals and objectives.	❑	❑	❑	❑	❑

	Risk Tolerance				
	A	B	C	D	E
17. An investment you made six months ago turned sour and currently is showing a 30% decline. How would you respond? a) Do nothing and wait for a rebound b) Sell and cut your losses c) Buy more and dollar-cost-average your investment	❑	❑	❑		
18. Given the following situations, which would you choose? a) $1,000 cash now b) A 50% chance of winning $3,000 c) A 20% chance of winning $10,000 d) A 10% chance of winning $25,000	❑	❑	❑	❑	
19. If you were faced with two potential gains, which would you choose? a) A 100% chance to win $2,000 b) An 80% chance to win $3,000	❑	❑			
20. If you were faced with two potential losses, which would you choose? a) A 100% chance to lose $2,000 b) An 80% chance to lose $3,000	❑	❑			
21. Which situation would you prefer? a) Investments in money market vehicles, only to see that aggressive growth stocks appreciated by 40% during the year. b) Investments in aggressive growth stocks which appreciate very little during the year.	❑	❑			
22. Which situation would you prefer? a) Investment in money market vehicles that prevented you from losing 40% of your capital in a market correction. b) Investment in equities that double your money.	❑	❑			
23. In an inflationary environment, hard assets such as precious metals, collectibles, and real estate are expected to keep pace with inflation. You currently hold all of your assets in money market vehicles. Most market analysts and economists predict inflation will skyrocket next year. What would you do? a) Continue to hold your money market vehicles. b) Sell half of your money market vehicles and buy some hard assets. c) Sell all of your money market vehicles and buy hard assets. d) Sell all of your money market vehicles and buy hard assets and borrow additional money to buy more.	❑	❑	❑	❑	

	Risk Tolerance				
	A	B	C	D	E

24. Based on a double-digit inflation forecast for the next several years and massive government deficits how would you invest? ❏ ❏ ❏ ❏ ❏
a) Buy Canada Savings Bonds and Treasury Bills.
b) Buy long-term GICs, TDs, and money market instruments.
c) Buy long-term equity based mutual funds.
d) Buy equities and real estate.
e) Buy gold and precious metals.

25. You receive an inside tip from a close friend on a junior oil company that could be a takeover candidate. If the deal goes through you could make a lot of money, but if it fails you could lose a substantial sum. How much stock would you buy? ❏ ❏ ❏ ❏ ❏
a) NONE
b) $2,000
c) $5,000
d) $10,000
e) $25,000

Scoring

Here are the points earned by each response:

1	A 1	B 2	C 3	D 4	E 5	14	A 5	B 4	C 3	D 2	E 1
2	A 1	B 2	C 3	D 4	E 5	15	A 5	B 4	C 3	D 2	E 1
3	A 1	B 2	C 3	D 4	E 5	16	A 5	B 4	C 3	D 2	E 1
4	A 1	B 2	C 3	D 4	E 5	17	A 1	B 3	C 5		
5	A 1	B 2	C 3	D 4	E 5	18	A 1	B 3	C 4	D 5	
6	A 1	B 2	C 3	D 4	E 5	19	A 1	B 5			
7	A 1	B 2	C 3	D 4	E 5	20	A 5	B 1			
8	A 1	B 2	C 3	D 4	E 5	21	A 1	B 5			
9	A 1	B 2	C 3	D 4	E 5	22	A 1	B 5			
10	A 5	B 4	C 3	D 2	E 1	23	A 1	B 2	C 3	D 5	
11	A 5	B 4	C 3	D 2	E 1	24	A 1	B 2	C 3	D 4	E 5
12	A 5	B 4	C 3	D 2	E 1	25	A 1	B 2	C 3	D 4	E 5
13	A 5	B 4	C 3	D 2	E 1						

Total Score: _____
What kind of investment personality do you have?

Your Investment Personality Score Results
25-50 points
Very Conservative (Risk-Avoider)

If you scored 50 or fewer points, you are likely a very conservative investor. Safety of capital is very important to you, so risk is something you prefer to minimize or even avoid altogether. Variability in your investments is not something you enjoy, and you are prepared to accept lower returns as a trade-off for being sure your capital is guaranteed. The types of products you favour are probably savings accounts and cash equivalents such as money market funds, T-Bills, CSBs, TDs, and GICs.

51-75 points
Conservative (Risk-Minimizer)

At 51 to 75 points, you are still quite conservative. Instead of totally avoiding risk, however, you are likely comfortable with a small bit of risk, but will try to minimize its effect. You favour the same products as the Very Conservative personality, but would also be comfortable with bonds and debentures, preferred shares, and some high-quality blue-chip common shares for income.

76-100 points
Growth-Oriented (Risk-Blender)

Between 76 and 100 points, you are a "risk-blender." You are less conservative than those who scored lower points, and you would like to see some growth in your portfolio. You will always have some conservative products in your portfolio. You will also want to have a good selection of common shares or mutual funds invested in stocks to achieve the desired growth in your investments. You might include a wide range of investment vehicles in your portfolio, including aggressive common stocks, foreign and global equity mutual funds, some convertible shares, warrants, and perhaps a tax-sheltered investment.

101-125 points
Speculative (Risk-Taker)

The highest scores on this questionnaire indicate that you are not only comfortable with risk, but also welcome it when you believe it will create the conditions for achieving the growth you seek. While your portfolio will have some cash and blue-chip stocks in it, you may lean towards more speculative common shares, options, futures, precious metals, certain higher-risk real estate investments, and special situations.

Your Investment Personality Profile gives you an indication of your comfort and tolerance levels with different types of investments, but will the financial vehicles associated with your "type" be the ones that will help you meet your retire-

ment objectives? To help you answer this question, consider the
Investment Pyramid of risks and rewards in Chart 12–2.

Investment Personality Questionnaire Analysis
Your investment decisions are personal and will reflect your
goals, needs, attitudes, and philosophy.

The 3 factors that will have the greatest impact on the
amount of money you accumulate for retirement are:

- How much money you save.
- How long your money is invested.
- What rate of return you earn on your investments.

The first and most important step is to identify your goals:
How much you'll need and when you'll need it.

The second step is to understand your comfort zone or
tolerance for risk.

The Investment Pyramid

One way to understand your personal investment profile is to
evaluate the type of investments that would be suitable for you.
Take a couple of minutes to study types of investments at each
level of the pyramid in Chart 12–2. Notice how the risk/reward
relationship changes as you move up and down the pyramid.

Level 1
The investment pyramid represents your personal financial
plan. At the bottom of the plan are all the investments offering
safety of capital. You will see that your chequing and savings
accounts are listed here, as well as term deposits, and guaranteed investments certificates, life insurance, and your home.
Since they offer little risk and generally lower returns, they are
considered to be the foundation of virtually every personal
financial plan.

Level 2
Moving up the pyramid, the second level holds securities that
fulfill the objectives of income and moderate growth. These are
corporate bonds and debentures, common stocks and preferred
stocks, income-producing real estate, and a variety of mutual
funds. Your potential returns are likely to be a little better for the
additional risk.

Level 3
Moving further up the pyramid, you encounter investments that involve a higher degree of uncertainty — and, in some cases complexity. These include investments in common shares of lesser-known companies, in preferred shares and debentures that are convertible into common shares of the same companies, and warrants and options. This level also includes specialty mutual funds and speculative real estate such as tax shelters.

THE INVESTMENT PYRAMID
Chart 12–2

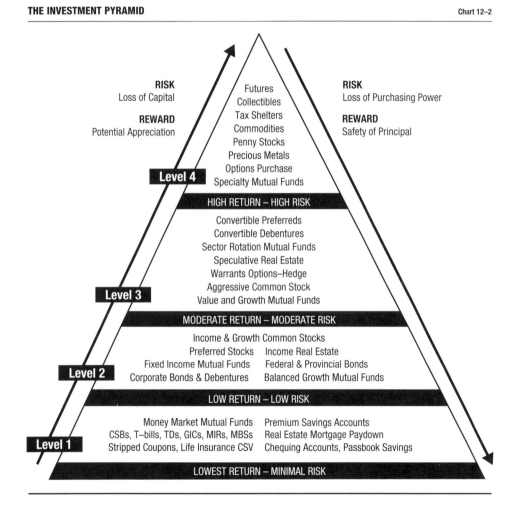

Level 4

There are fewer vehicles as we climb the pyramid to the top where the greatest potential returns exist — alongside the greatest risks to your investment capital! Precious metals, such as gold and silver, are in this category, as well as financial and commodity futures, penny stocks, and collectibles like antiques, jewelry, china, art, and rugs.

The Relationship Between Investment Reward and Risk

As you move up the arrow on the left side of the Investment Pyramid in Chart 12–2, you risk greater loss of capital, but you increase your potential to experience the reward of capital appreciation. For example, moving from the safety of investments on Level 1 to blue-chip common stocks in Level 2 increases not only your risk but also your potential for growth.

The arrow pointing down the right side of the pyramid shows that as you descend, you are increasing the risk of a loss of purchasing power in your capital due to inflation. At the same time, however, you are increasingly rewarded with safety of your principal. As you purchase investments further down the pyramid, you will recall that almost all of the investments on Level 1 guarantee your capital.

Chart 12–3 below shows the pyramid idea another way. Using four levels for the pyramid on the left, the investments are divided into four categories corresponding to different investment objectives. The pyramid to the right is inverted to show the trade-off between rewards and risks.

In order to achieve the maximum reward — as indicated at the top of the pyramid in Chart 12–3 — you are likely taking the greatest risk by investing in securities that offer the potential of aggressive growth. At the bottom, your risk-free cash reserves and income investments will reward you with only modest returns.

It is important to recognize that you don't have to participate on all levels on the pyramid. The Chart is designed to encourage you to decide whether the investments you are comfortable with are appropriate to your objectives.

A key factor in your comfort with risk is your knowledge about investments. With a little more exposure to these concepts, you may decide that you want to become a more active investor. At that point, your comfort level with risk would pre-sumably increase. And, as your comfort level changes, so should your investment habits.

BALANCING YOUR INVESTMENT STRATEGY   Chart 12–3

Degrees of Investment Risk/Reward	Your Investment Personality	Your Portfolio Objectives
AGGRESSIVE GROWTH	RISK–TAKER	HIGH RISK/ REWARD
MODERATE GROWTH AND INCOME	RISK–BLENDER	MODERATE RISK/REWARD
LOW GROWTH AND INCOME	RISK–MINIMIZER	LOW RISK/ REWARD
RESERVES - INCOME INVESTMENTS	RISK–AVOIDER	VIRTUALLY NO RISK/REWARD

Asset Allocation

Up to 90% of the result a typical portfolio returns is based on asset allocation; only 10% is based on market timing and securi-ty selection. The solution for a successful investment experience is to discover your investment personality; know your invest-ment time frame; allocate resources to suit your personality across each asset class; and then leave things alone. Of course there will be the need to rebalance the percentages allocated to each asset class from time to time. Essentially if you were design-ing a portfolio based on a **rest of your life plan** scenario then Step 1 would be to asset allocate and Step 2 would be to rebal-ance the portfolio as required. The following depicts the asset classes and types of investments:

ASSET ALLOCATION   Table 12–4

Major Objective	Asset Class	Investment Selection
Liquidity	*Reserves*	*T-Bills*
Income	*Debt*	*Bonds*
Growth	*Equity*	*Stocks*

ASSET ALLOCATION AND INVESTMENT OPTIONS				Table 12–5
	Risk Minimizer	Risk Avoider	Risk Blender	Risk Taker
Cash	5%	5%	5%	_%
GICs, TDs	60	40	10	5
Bonds	25	30	30	20
Equities (Canadian)	10	15	40	55
Equities (Foreign)	–	10	15	20
Total	100%	100%	100%	100%

Investment Time Frames

The most important thing the investor needs to know after determining his/her investment personality profile is his/her investment time frame. The following depicts several time frames and the appropriate asset classes and investment selections for each.

It is imperative to match your time frame with the appropriate asset class. No matter what your investment personality would permit, you must match maturities to allow the selected investments to deliver their full potential reward. For instance if you had $50,000 to invest but you only had a one-year time frame, then the appropriate asset class would be reserves and the investments

Time Frame	Asset Class	Investment Selection
1 Year	Reserves	Cash, T-Bills, GICs, TDs
2 Years	Debt	Short-term Bonds, Preferreds
3-5 Years	Balanced	T-Bills, Bonds, Stocks
6+ Years	Equity	Stocks, Equity Mutual Funds
Lifetime		Knowledge

could be any cash or equivalent investment that matures in one year or less. Similarly, if you were investing for your retirement ten years in the future, then equities would be an appropriate asset class for a portion of your money dependent upon your investment personality profile. Much of what we teach in our programs is based on long-term planning or what we call a rest of your life plan. Table 12–5 gives you a range of possible asset allocation strategies to match the four investment personality profiles.

Market Timing

The odds against trying to **beat the market** by security selection and market timing are substantial. A market timer would have to be successful about 70% of the time for this strategy to pay off. Why is it so tough to beat the market on a consistent basis? There are three main reasons:

"When is the best time to buy stock? When you have the money!"
— John Templeton

- Bull markets last longer than bear markets; the ratio is about 3:1.
- Stocks go up over time more than they go down as companies grow.
- Most upward market performance occurs in unpredictable spurts; no one rings a bell indicating when to get in or out.

You can see from the foregoing why we recommend an asset allocation strategy that fits your investment personality and that once you're invested to basically leave the portfolio alone. With age comes wisdom and some of the oldest and wisest market seers, such as Warren Buffet and John Templeton, have chosen to seek out value in their investments. They know that market cycles repeat with regularity and that each new cycle surpasses the last like a series of waves occurring four and five years apart.

Is This the Right Time?

Most investors always focus on the negative aspects of the market and things that can go wrong rather than the positive aspects and what could go right. The media don't help this situation either, because they focus on the negatives rather than the positives. After all — sensationalism sells! It's tough to convince people against their will. The business of investing is about reality, both present and future.

Market timing does not work for large institutions let alone the typical investor. Studies have shown that even the most successful professional market timers add very little additional return compared with those who lose substantially more by underperforming against the market indices. A buy and hold strategy is the best

Market Timing —
Turning time into money

129

strategy for most investors. The average investor who tries to be a market timer almost always fails!

Canadians — A Nation of Savers

"Forbes magazine annually lists the wealthiest 400 people in the world. Every one of them made money in one of two ways: ownership of real estate or ownership of great companies."

Generally speaking most Canadians prefer to deal with an advisor who is more conservative than they are. Canadians come by this trait naturally; we are a nation of savers, whereas the typical American citizens are investors. Why this difference? Much of it has to do with social security and medical coverage. Canada has been fortunate to provide excellent programs for its senior population, whereas the programs in the U.S. don't come close to matching ours. Therefore their citizens have had to be much more aggressive in their financial planning.

C A N A D I A N ?
A M E R I C A N !

It is in the psyche of most Canadians to adopt a very conservative "Can I?" approach biased to savings versus investing. Americans have an "I Can!" attitude and have taken a much more aggressive stance with their investments, which they have had to by necessity, to reach their retirement goals.

Risk Capital

The economies of all great democratic nations were built with two ingredients — risk capital and sweat equity (a plentiful supply of cheap labour.) The lenders of risk capital expect a greater reward than they would get from a fixed-income investment such as a GIC, otherwise the world would be upside down.

Your primary goal is to create a wealth system to look after you at retirement. Capital invested in great companies should produce enough income to outgrow your living costs. Not all investments

Greater risks for greater rewards

are perfect. However, if you were to diversify by building a port-folio of shares in great companies or by purchasing a mutual fund that invested in 50 to 100 or more of these companies, your wealth management system should look after you for the rest of your life.

People don't buy what you know; they buy what you believe. My core belief is in the repetitive nature of cycles. Everything in life has a cycle: business, economics, government elections, and global activity, — moon and tide, day and night, right down to the reproduction cycle of life itself. History has shown that the stock market is also cyclical; that the rhythm of the markets is repetitive.

"The lowest ebb is the turn of the tide."
— Longfellow

Faith in the future based on the belief of the occurrence of ever increasing cyclical markets is the secret to becoming a successful investor. Knowledgeable investors know that the greatest risk in the 21st century will be to outlive one's capital if one's invest-ment portfolio is not asset allocated with a significant percentage in equities.

Wealth Accumulation

Virtually all great companies grow over time through increasing sales and revenue growth, through mergers, acquisitions and takeovers, and through global diversification. As a result most companies' earnings, dividends, and stock prices also increase over time. The formula for wealth accumulation is to own shares in these great companies. Each one of these companies apply risk capital + sweat equity + knowledge equity to = wealth accumula-tion to ensure their success.

The greatest risk most investors face is the possibility of outliv-ing their capital. And the major long-term risk this century has

The Market Forces

131

been not owning shares in quality companies. The real risk has been not taking any risk. The secret to a long-term successful investment experience is to own shares in great companies whose products and services you use every day. These companies increase their dividends from year to year, thus providing long-term growth in income, which is the ultimate inflation killer.

In our programs I often ask if anyone in the room does not have a telephone? Of course, they all do! Then I ask if anyone in the group is planning not to have a telephone next year? Once again, they all plan to keep their telephones. Then I ask if their telephone bills are higher or lower than last year. What do you think the answer is to that question? I ask the same series of question regarding ownership of bank stocks and pipeline utilities, and question who receives the profits these companies make? Is the profit retained in the business? Is it paid to employees? Is it paid to shareholders with dividends? Is it a combination of all of these? Let's take a look at BCE Inc. to review an actual corporate history.

Ownership in Great Companies

The only way to ensure the growth of your capital is by ownership of shares in companies. Your future purchasing power is derived from dividend income from great companies whose products and services, you and I use every day.

Great companies stock prices increase over time.
Great companies earnings increase over time.
Great companies dividends increase over time.

"Faith is the force of life."
— Tolstoy

Let's take a look at BCE Inc. in Table 12–6. Assume you bought BCE Inc. at $22.375 in January 1983, when the dividend was $2.08. To obtain the yield of 9.30% at that time simply divide the dividend of $2.08 by the price of $22.375. I might add that you could have purchased other fixed-income investments such as a guaranteed investment certificate (GIC) to yield over 11% at that time.

Now fast forward ten years. The price of BCE Inc. is now $44.25 an increase of 98%; the dividend is now $2.64 an increase of 27%; and the yield has dropped to 5.97% a decrease of 36% to reflect interest rates and stock prices in 1993. But what would your current yield be relative to your original price ten years ago? Simply divide the current dividend of $2.64 by the purchase price in 1983 to obtain your current yield of 11.80%. To derive a fair comparison to interest income this yield is increased or grossed up by 25% to show a comparative interest equivalent yield of 14.75%

Note: Interest income is fully taxed at your marginal rate. Dividend income is reduced by the federal dividend tax credit, which is offered to encourage you to invest in Canadian corporations. To calculate tax, you gross-up your dividends by 25%. Net federal tax payable is calculated by using this grossed-up amount and deducting a tax credit of 16.66% of the actual dividend received or 13.33% of the grossed-up dividend — from the grossed-up dividend provincial tax is then calculated on the net federal tax payable.

Let's get back to our example of BCE Inc. Since most of your financial decisions will depend on what your investment earns, what return would you have realized on a GIC purchased in 1993? Certainly no where near the 14.75% return you are currently receiving on BCE Inc. One other very important point bears mentioning. Suppose you purchased a five year GIC for $10,000 in 1983 at 12% and renewed it for another five-year GIC in 1988 at 10% versus the purchase of $10,000 worth of BCE Inc. What would your status be in 1993? The GIC would still be worth $10,000 in 1993 and a new five-year term would yield about 9%. Ownership in BCE Inc. stock has increase in value by 98% to $19,800 and it currently yields 14.75% based on the original purchase price in 1983.

Now let's take a look at Table 12–7 and update BCE Inc. statistics to 1996. The capital gain on the stock has increased by 191% and assuming a $10,000 investment in 1983, you could now sell the stock for $29,100. The grossed-up yield on the original purchase price is 15.43% Had you chosen the GIC route, your original capital would still be worth $10,000 and the yield on a five year GIC in 1996 was about 5.25%. This evidence is pretty powerful — need we say more?

"We like to buy businesses. We don't like to sell, and we expect the relationships to last a lifetime."
— Warren Buffett

BCE INC.			Table 12–6
	Jan. 1983	**Jan. 1993**	**% Change**
Price	22.375	44.25	98%
Dividend	2.08	2.64	27%
Yield	9.30%	5.97%	-36%
Yield on 1983 Cost Price	11.80%		
Dividend Gross-Up — 25%	2.95%		
Comparative Interest Equivalent Yield	14.75%		

BCE Inc.   Table 12–7

	Jan. 1983	Jan. 1996	% Change
Price	22.375	65.30	191%
Dividend	2.08	2.76	33%
Yield	9.30%	4.32%	-54%
Yield on 1983 Cost Price	12.34%		
Dividend Gross-Up — 25%	3.09%		
Comparative Interest Equivalent Yield	15.43%		

Chaotic Risk Aversion Psychosis (CRAP)

"Money, the life blood of the nation, corrupts and stagnates in its veins, unless a proper circulation, its motion and its heat maintains."
Dean Swift

The word crap means nonsense, dirt, or rubbish; to crap out means to be unsuccessful, to withdraw from the game. CRAP is a dreaded disease that has prevented more people from reaching their goals and dreams than any other factor.

Probably the greatest entrapment ever fostered on the Canadian public is the mindset created by the $60,000 Canadian Deposit Insurance Corporation guarantee. This insurance covers bank, trust, and loan company deposits such as chequing, savings, premium saving accounts; term deposits (TD), and guaranteed investment certificates (GIC); money orders, drafts, and traveller's cheques.

The insurance provides the investor with a false sense of security. Why? Let's assume an investor in the highest tax bracket purchases a five-year GIC yielding 6% and inflation is averaging 4%:

Pre-tax Yield	6.00%
Less Taxes @ 50%	3.00%
After-tax Yield	3.00%
Less Inflation	4.00%
Purchasing Power Loss	-1.00%

The greatest risk the investor faces is the possibility of outliving one's capital, therefore you must create an income that can outgrow your living costs. Only one asset can do that consistently — ownership of shares in great companies such as the BCE Inc. example we have discussed.

Why the Urgency?

How old are you today? How much money have you earned in your lifetime so far? How much have you managed to save for

Lack of planning can turn your dreams sour

your future? If you are like most Canadians Tables 12–8 and 12–9 can be downright depressing when you realize how much money has passed through your hands and how little you have to show for it. But don't despair. The more important question is, "How much will you earn between now and your retirement, and how much of these earnings will you be willing to save?"

The choices you make today regarding how you invest what you save can make the difference between becoming a have or a have-not in the future. If you're like most Canadians you know you should begin to invest your hard-earned savings, but you haven't got a clue where to start. Fear not — what's required is a partnership! We discussed this at length in Part One and Part Two. In the next chapter we will review why most investors need financial advisors.

"Tough times never last, tough people do."
— Robert Schuller

135

HOW MUCH HAVE YOU EARNED IN YOUR LIFETIME SO FAR?   Table 12–8

(Based on starting work at age 25 and working to age 65)

Age	Years of Work	$2,000	$3,000	$4,000	$5,000	Monthly Cheques Spent	Monthly Cheques Left
26	1	$24,000	$36,000	$48,000	$60,000	12	480
27	2	48,000	72,000	96,000	120,000	24	468
28	3	72,000	108,000	144,000	180,000	36	456
29	4	96,000	144,000	192,000	240,000	48	444
30	5	120,000	180,000	240,000	300,000	60	432
31	6	144,000	216,000	288,000	360,000	72	420
32	7	168,000	252,000	336,000	420,000	84	408
33	8	192,000	288,000	384,000	480,000	96	396
34	9	216,000	324,000	432,000	540,000	108	384
35	10	240,000	360,000	480,000	600,000	120	372
36	11	264,000	396,000	528,000	660,000	132	360
37	12	288,000	432,000	576,000	720,000	144	348
38	13	312,000	468,000	624,000	780,000	156	336
39	14	336,000	504,000	672,000	840,000	168	324
40	15	360,000	540,000	720,000	900,000	180	312
41	16	384,000	576,000	768,000	960,000	192	300
42	17	408,000	612,000	816,000	1,020,000	204	288
43	18	432,000	648,000	864,000	1,080,000	216	276
44	19	456,000	684,000	912,000	1,140,000	228	264
45	20	480,000	720,000	960,000	1,200,000	240	252
46	21	504,000	756,000	1,008,000	1,260,000	252	240
47	22	528,000	792,000	1,056,000	1,320,000	264	228
48	23	552,000	828,000	1,104,000	1,380,000	276	216
49	24	576,000	864,000	1,152,000	1,440,000	288	204
50	25	600,000	900,000	1,200,000	1,500,000	300	192
51	26	624,000	936,000	1,248,000	1,560,000	312	180
52	27	648,000	972,000	1,296,000	1,620,000	324	168
53	28	672,000	1,008,000	1,344,000	1,680,000	336	156
54	29	696,000	1,044,000	1,392,000	1,740,000	348	144
55	30	720,000	1,080,000	1,440,000	1,800,000	360	132
56	31	744,000	1,116,000	1,488,000	1,860,000	372	120
57	32	768,000	1,152,000	1,536,000	1,920,000	384	108
58	33	792,000	1,188,000	1,584,000	1,980,000	396	96
59	34	816,000	1,224,000	1,632,000	2,040,000	408	84
60	35	840,000	1,260,000	1,680,000	2,100,000	420	72
61	36	864,000	1,296,000	1,728,000	2,160,000	432	60
62	37	888,000	1,332,000	1,776,000	2,220,000	444	48
63	38	912,000	1,368,000	1,824,000	2,280,000	456	36
64	39	936,000	1,404,000	1,872,000	2,340,000	468	24
65	40	960,000	1,440,000	1,920,000	2,400,000	480	12

"The past, the present, and the future are really one — they are today!"
— Stowe

136

HOW MUCH WILL YOU EARN BETWEEN NOW AND AGE 65?

Table 12–9

Years	Monthly Income					
	$2,000	$3,000	$4,000	$5,000	$7,500	$10,000
21	$1,080,000	$1,620,000	$2,160,000	$2,700,000	$4,050,000	$5,400,000
22	1,056,000	1,584,000	2,112,000	2,640,000	3,960,000	5,280,000
23	1,032,000	1,548,000	2,064,000	2,580,000	3,870,000	5,160,000
24	1,008,000	1,512,000	2,016,000	2,520,000	3,780,000	5,040,000
25	984,000	1,476,000	1,968,000	2,460,000	3,690,000	4,920,000
26	960,000	1,440,000	1,920,000	2,400,000	3,600,000	4,800,000
27	936,000	1,404,000	1,872,000	2,340,000	3,510,000	4,680,000
28	912,000	1,368,000	1,824,000	2,280,000	3,420,000	4,560,000
29	888,000	1,332,000	1,776,000	2,220,000	3,330,000	4,440,000
30	864,000	1,296,000	1,728,000	2,160,000	3,240,000	4,320,000
31	840,000	1,260,000	1,680,000	2,100,000	3,150,000	4,200,000
32	816,000	1,224,000	1,632,000	2,040,000	3,060,000	4,080,000
33	792,000	1,188,000	1,584,000	1,980,000	2,970,000	3,960,000
34	768,000	1,152,000	1,536,000	1,920,000	2,880,000	3,840,000
35	744,000	1,116,000	1,488,000	1,860,000	2,790,000	3,720,000
36	720,000	1,080,000	1,440,000	1,800,000	2,700,000	3,600,000
37	696,000	1,044,000	1,392,000	1,740,000	2,610,000	3,480,000
38	672,000	1,008,000	1,344,000	1,680,000	2,520,000	3,360,000
39	648,000	972,000	1,296,000	1,620,000	2,430,000	3,240,000
40	624,000	936,000	1,248,000	1,560,000	2,340,000	3,120,000
41	600,000	900,000	1,200,000	1,500,000	2,250,000	3,000,000
42	576,000	864,000	1,152,000	1,440,000	2,160,000	2,880,000
43	552,000	828,000	1,104,000	1,380,000	2,070,000	2,760,000
44	528,000	792,000	1,056,000	1,320,000	1,980,000	2,640,000
45	504,000	756,000	1,008,000	1,260,000	1,890,000	2,520,000
46	480,000	720,000	960,000	1,200,000	1,800,000	2,400,000
47	456,000	684,000	912,000	1,140,000	1,710,000	2,280,000
48	432,000	648,000	864,000	1,080,000	1,620,000	2,160,000
49	408,000	612,000	816,000	1,020,000	1,530,000	2,040,000
50	384,000	576,000	768,000	960,000	1,440,000	1,920,000
51	360,000	540,000	720,000	900,000	1,350,000	1,800,000
52	336,000	504,000	672,000	840,000	1,260,000	1,680,000
53	312,000	468,000	624,000	780,000	1,170,000	1,560,000
54	288,000	432,000	576,000	720,000	1,080,000	1,440,000
55	264,000	396,000	528,000	660,000	990000	1,320,000
56	240,000	360,000	480,000	600,000	900000	1,200,000
57	216,000	324,000	432,000	540,000	810000	1,080,000
58	192,000	288,000	384,000	480,000	720000	960000
59	168,000	252,000	336,000	420,000	630000	840000
60	144,000	216,000	288,000	360,000	540000	720000
61	120,000	180,000	240,000	300,000	450000	600000
62	96,000	144,000	192,000	240,000	360000	480000
63	72,000	108,000	144,000	180,000	270000	360000
64	48,000	72,000	96,000	120,000	180000	240000
65	24,000	36,000	48,000	60,000	90000	120000

"The journey of a 1,000 miles starts with a single step."
— Chinese Proverb

Thirteen

Putting It All Together

THERE IS A PERCEPTION AMONG MANY INVESTORS THAT BIGGER IS better; therefore many investors look no further than the old four pillars of the financial service community. These large institutions obviously have the depth of resources, including people and capital, to provide exhaustive research, including quantitative and qualitative fundamental analysis and technical analysis. They have the in-house support staff to enable them to offer one-stop shopping for their clients, and many have global partnerships or correspondent networks to provide access to world markets.

Does this mean the independent planner/advisor can't compete? On the contrary, many independents can do an even better job of providing research and service. Because they are independent they can buy the best brains available all over the world. Unlike the large institution, which is often locked into a monolithic structure, the independent can tap the very best of the world's resources to place at the investor's disposal. The high-tech, high-touch communications revolution affords everyone the same opportunity to compete on a level playing field.

Full-Service Dealer versus Single-Family Agent

Most financial institutions are biased to their own product offerings. The bank or trust company wants to sell its mutual funds and fixed-income products such as GICs and term deposits; the life insurance agent usually represents one family of funds; the largest independent mutual fund family in Canada has its own direct sales force and prior to 1997 could only sell its own products. Now their agents can sell a few other families of funds as well. Full-service dealers such as stockbrokers or mutual fund advisors often represent a complete range of families of funds, and, in the case of stockbrokers, a whole range of other products as well.

So which type of agent is best for you? For some investors too much choice could lead to indecision. Some folks feel that a single-family mutual fund company would not offer enough diversification. There are two thoughts you may want to consider regarding this quandary. The first is, "It is better to own the wrong mutual fund at the right time than the right mutual fund at the wrong time." The second is, "An experienced, trustworthy, reputable, planner/advisor who represents a single family of funds is more valuable than a full-service agent who does not have the characteristics and traits you are looking for in a partnership."

Big Brand Name versus Boutique

Most investors feel a significant degree of comfort when dealing with a large institution. Each of the bank-owned brokerages do very well with image conscious investors. In reality the investor is just as safe dealing with a boutique or even an advisor who runs a practice as a sole proprietorship. The reason for this is that the securities you own are held by a third party and segregated. As well there are the numerous safeguards for the investor described in Chapter 10.

Studies have shown that investors rank advisors and investment firms about equally when making a decision to invest. Major factors that attract investors to either the advisor or the company are as follows:

Advisor	*Large Company*
Trustworthy	Trustworthy — money secure
Knowledgeable advice	Offers broad range of services
Reference or referral	Competitive service fees
Personalized contact and service operation	Convenience — storefront
Portfolio management	One-stop shopping

Packaged Money Approach

Mutual funds have become the investment of choice of the baby-boom generation. The pressures of work and the demand on time for today's typical investor lead most to the line of least resistance — using a packaged money approach to save and invest for their futures. Whether you decide to use mutual funds or individual securities to build your portfolio, it is important to understand the various managerial styles.

Professional Money Management Styles

Once you find an advisor you are comfortable with, try to determine his/her management style. There are many professional styles of money management. Every professional money manager employs at least one money management style and more often a combination. There are three types of money management personalities:

- Market timers
- Growth investors
- Value investors

Make sure your advisor's style and personality suit your personality and way of thinking.

Bottom-Up Style (Value Investor)
The advisor seeks undervalued securities with little regard for overall economic and market conditions. He/she select stocks trading at discount to book value and low price-earnings multiple and is prepared to sit with the selected security for many years in order to recognize the stock's full potential.

Top-Down Style (Group or Sector Rotator)
The advisor analyses the macro and micro economic trends and market forecasts then selects attractive groups to participate in, with stocks that are the leaders and show the most promise in their industry.

Diversified Growth Style
The advisor combines the bottom-up and the top-down styles to select a cross section of securities poised for above average growth over the intermediate to long term. He/she selects stocks based on fundamentals with

Don't put all your eggs in one basket.

141

above average increases in cash flow, revenues, earnings per share, or market share.

Balanced Growth Style (Asset Allocation)
The advisor combines the bottom-up and top-down styles and measures risk/reward by mathematical analyses of various classes of common shares, preferred shares, bonds and debentures, and a variety of money market assets in order to reduce risk. He/she uses fundamental analysis of economic growth, interest rates, and market analysis of securities.

Hedged Style
The advisor may use any of the above approaches individually or together, including derivatives to enhance portfolio performance. A typical strategy that provides a less volatile performance is selling options on securities held in the portfolio. The premiums earned on the options provide steady income, but the hedged style also precludes the possibility of superior capital gains if the underlying stock is called away should the purchaser exercise the option.

Market Timers
This type of advisor uses technical analysis based on price trends for individual stocks, or stock group, or market as a whole. Really good market timers are a rare breed and very hard to find.

In addition to learning as much as you can about the advisor's investment philosophy, strategy, and style, look for a verifiable long-term record of performance over one, three, five, and ten years, encompassing both good and bad marketing periods.

There are two potentially fatal flaws that can destroy the best laid plans:

"No one has ever lost money in the history of the stock market, if he/she stayed committed to the original plan he/she intended to complete in the first place."
— Graydon Watters

• Do not buy last year's hero, it is likely to be next year's bum. Many investors buy the best performing fund from the past year. If you were to use past performance in your investment decisions then buy last year's bum; it's likely to be next year's hero.
• Establish market benchmarks such as the Toronto Stock Exchange 300 Index to measure your performance. Recognize that managerial styles go in and out of favour.

Don't react too soon and be prepared to stick with the style when it falls out of favour if it suits your personality.

How to Monitor the Performance of Your Money Manager

How can you measure the performance of your professional money manager? I recommend using the investment industry's common performance criteria for a complete market cycle of approximately four to six years. If your financial planner is performing well, his/her performance over the period of this market cycle will

1. exceed the Consumer Price Index by 3% to 5% compounded per year
2. outperform the Toronto Stock Exchange Composite Index by 4% to 6% compounded per year
3. perform in the top quartile amongst his/her peer group of managers
4. outperform the Toronto Stock Exchange Composite Index during all down years

MANAGEMENT STYLE — EQUITIES Chart 13–1

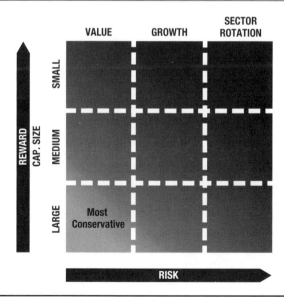

Good Old-Fashioned Common Sense

- It is much easier to buy than to sell an investment. Most investors lose money because they don't know when to sell.
- Don't let small losses become big losses.
- If the information about a company sounds too good to be true, it probably is.
- Be wary of initial public offerings (IPOs.) Know who the promoter is and how well researched and accurate the information on the company is. Above all — read the prospectus!
- Never begrudge paying an investment professional for good sound advice. Alternatively, don't pay for advice you don't need.
- Survival for the 21st century will necessitate lifelong learning — challenge yourself to read a minimum of one financial book per year.
- The best approach to investing for 99% of all investors is
  - know your investment personality and risk tolerance profile
  - know your investment time frame
  - structure your portfolio across all asset classes
  - remove as many market timing decisions as possible
  - make subtle shifts only when necessary to maintain your asset allocation percentages

"Common sense is instinct, and enough of it is genius."
— H. W. Shaw

Mutual Fund Smarts

- Look for a manager who has a good track record and a lower than average management expense ratio (MER).
- With 1,500 mutual funds to choose from narrow your range to one to three smart families of funds.
- You are usually better off negotiating a small-front load than purchasing a back-loaded fund that may carry a trailer fee in perpetuity.
- When your mutual fund assets exceed $250,000, you might consider the services of an investment counsellor within the same family of funds, if available, or seek out an independent counselling firm to manage your portfolio. You should be able to save 1% to 2% per annum, which could easily amount to an additional six figures in your pocket over time.

*Mutual funds can greatly reduce your risk and workload
of investment decisions and portfolio management.*

Sudden Windfall or Inheritance

It is estimated that as much as $1 trillion will be handed down from one generation to the next during the next 12 to 15 years. Chances are you may be one of the lucky recipients. Therefore it is best you understand now what to expect at that time.

Emotions will run extremely high, anxiety will set in, and worry about blowing or losing this new found wealth will haunt the recipient, especially during the initial days and weeks. The best advice I can suggest to face this unsettled period is to lock up the capital for a period of three months perhaps in a 90-day treasury bill or a term deposit. Give yourself space; time to reflect and plan for the future. Follow this checklist with your new found wealth:

1. Use the tools in this book to seek out a financial planner/ advisor.
2. Beware of well-meaning relatives and friends. If the sum is substantial, many of them will want a piece of the action.
3. If you do lend money to friends or relatives, put the transactions in writing and insist on collateral to cover the loans.
4. Pay off all credit card debts.

145

5. Pay down your mortgage if appropriate.
6. Use income splitting where possible to minimize tax.

Always remember that **money is simply a giggle that allows you to do outrageous things**. If you make it your god it will destroy you! Sit back, find the balance that fits your personality and comfort zone, and above all — enjoy your money!

Why Investors Need Financial Advisors

"80% of Canadians don't feel they have good money management and investment skills, yet only 50% of them have a financial advisor."

Let's take a moment to summarize why investors need financial advisors.

- Fear and greed are the two major motivators that get most investors into trouble.
- Market timing does not work for the average investor.
- Investors get caught up with the psychology of markets and often make mistakes based on herd instinct, vogue, fads, etc.
- There are more mutual fund companies than stocks in the U.S. How does the average investor choose which are best?
- Doing nothing is in fact a decision and almost always the wrong thing to do. Many investors crap out!
- Most investors do not have the time, knowledge, temperament, and money to manage on their own.
- Choose adventure over safety. This implies ownership of shares in great companies.
- The critical skills are listening, feedback, coaching, counselling, mentoring, and tutoring to meet your needs and objectives. Ask yourself, honestly, would you invest on your own?
- Advisors determine their client's comfort zone, using tools such as the Investment Personality Questionnaire.
- Advisors identify their client's **needs** versus **wants**.
- Advisors empower their clients to accept responsibility for their futures.
- Advisors help manage their client's market stress levels.

How to Choose a Financial Advisor

This is what you have been leading up to and here you are. How do you choose the right advisor to help you accomplish your investment goals? Remember, next to your number one asset — your physical health — you are dealing with a very important asset

— your financial health. You cannot afford to make a major mistake.

As a prospective investor you should interview at least three financial advisors to see who best matches your personality requirements, needs, and goals. The most effective use of your time is to ask as many questions as possible during the initial interview. The following worksheet is a list of questions to help you through the interview to select this most important advisor relationship. It provides all of the ammunition you'll need to find and solidify a partnership. You need to feel comfortable in selecting one of the most important relationships in your life!

HOW TO CHOOSE A FINANCIAL ADVISOR — QUICK CHECKLIST   Worksheet 13–3

Is the advisor a good listener, in tune with your needs and concerns?

_____

_____

Does the advisor communicate in lay terms?

_____

_____

What are this advisor's educational qualifications and professional experience/credentials?

_____

_____

What licences, degrees, diplomas, and designations does the advisor hold?

_____

_____

How long has the advisor been in the business?

_____

_____

What was the advisor's previous occupation?

_____

_____

Is the advisor financially bonded and does he or she carry errors and omissions insurance?

_____

_____

Is there a record of past performance upon which you can base realistic expectations?

_____

_____

What's the average age of the advisor's clientele?

_____

_____

What types of clients does the advisor serve?

_____

_____

Will the advisor provide you with a list of references?

_____

_____

What is the financial planning process the advisor proposes to follow? Is it clearly presented to you, or do you find it confusing?

_____

_____

How does the advisor determine what investments suit your risk profile?

_____

_____

How does the advisor classify his/her investment style — value, growth, or sector rotator?

_____

_____

What type of report does this person prepare? Ask for a copy of a sample plan or portfolio.

_____

_____

Does the plan cover budgeting, debt management, estate planning, taxation, and investments?

_____

_____

Does the advisor have a particular area of client specialization?

_____

_____

What aspects of your financial needs will not be covered?

_____

_____

What type of products does the advisor recommend?

_____

_____

Is the advisor competent to give general advice in all types of investments, insurance, tax strategies, and estate planning?

_____

_____

148

Is the advisor tied into just one vendor or is he or she a multi-product agent?

_____

_____

Can the advisor tap into a network of special professional services? If so, which ones?

_____

_____

What role will the advisor play in the implementation of the proposed financial plan?

_____

_____

How does this person charge for services? (commission only? fee only? fee plus commission? fee-based?)

_____

_____

Are the fees and/or commissions fair and competitive?

_____

_____

If fee-based, does the advisor charge a flat fee, an hourly rate, a percentage of assets, or a combination?

_____

_____

If commission-based is the percentage negotiable?

_____

_____

How does the mutual fund manager get paid?

_____

_____

Does the advisor receive trailer commissions?

_____

_____

Does the advisor exercise due diligence to fully assess all potential risks as well as rewards of each proposed investment?

_____

_____

Will the advisor provide a letter of complete disclosure of all costs and any potential conflicts of interest?

_____

_____

"You are your greatest investment. The more you store in that mind of yours, the more you enrich your experience, the more people you meet, the more books you read, and the more places you visit, the greater is that investment in all that you are. Everything that you add to your peace of mind, and to your outlook upon life, is added capital that no one but yourself can dissipate."
— George Matthew Adams

149

What follow-up services does the advisor offer after the initial investments are made?

_____

_____

How often will you meet and how often is the portfolio reviewed?

_____

_____

Should the advisor become unavailable, who will be assigned to work with your plan?

_____

_____

_____

Where Do You Go from Here?

Choosing a financial intermediary is never a black or white decision — there are always shades of gray. As you have seen there are many factors to assess in choosing an advisor, and you should now be ready to develop a relationship. I wish you all of the best that life has to offer and much financial success, but most of all I hope you'll find that special partnership with a financial professional that you have always wanted.

A Client's Bill of Rights

1. I have the right to deal with an advisor I can trust.
2. I have the right to expect my advisor to put my interests first in all business transactions.
3. I have the right to expect my advisor to listen to me, to understand my needs and objectives, and to appreciate my tolerance for risk.
4. I have the right to deal with an advisor who will respect my confidentiality and my privacy.
5. I have the right to expect my advisor to develop a comprehensive financial plan to achieve my long-term goals.
6. I have the right to expect my advisor to implement my plan directly or to coordinate the activities of a network of professional specialists.
7. I have the right to expect my advisor to design an investment portfolio that will achieve long-term growth without undue risk.
8. I have the right to expect my advisor to keep me informed, both verbally and in writing, of my portfolio's performance in a clear and concise format.
9. I have the right to expect my advisor to be easily accessible most of the time and to return telephone calls promptly.
10. I have the right to deal with a top-notch professional who is respected by his/her peers, has recognized degrees and designations, has experience and technical competence, and adheres to ethical standards and practices.
11. I have the right to expect my advisor to provide me with continuing client education, and I further expect my advisor to be committed to a program of lifelong learning.
12. If I am not satisfied with the service I receive, I have the right to move my account to another advisor or firm.

Financial Intermediaries — Resource Directory

We greatly appreciate and acknowledge the Investors Association of Canada for their permission to use excerpts from their Resource Directory.

The Investors Association of Canada (IAC) is a nationally chartered association of individual investors. It is a non-profit organization. The primary objective of the IAC is to be a source of investor education by providing basic as well as timely investment information.

IAC communicates with its members mainly through its monthly publication, *Money Digest*, and offers an unbiased, generic overview of investment activity. Each issue provides an investment capsule on mortgages, fixed income, high-yield stock dividend, deposit rates, a mutual fund summary, and general interest articles.

For further information contact:
Investors Association of Canada (IAC)
26 Soho Street, Suite 380
Toronto On M5T 1Z7

Tel: (416) 340-1723
Fax: (416) 340-9202

Associations/Institutes

Your investment needs can be addressed by a variety of associations and institutions. Depending on your needs, one or more of the following associations/institutes may be able to help you.

Cdn. Assn. of Financial Planners	439 University Ave., #1710	Toronto	ON	M5G 1Y8	(416) 593-6592
Canadian Assn. of Retired Persons	27 Queen St. E., #1304	Toronto	ON	M5C 2M6	(416) 363-8748
Canadian Bankers Association	Box 348, Commerce Court W., 30th	Toronto	ON	M5L 1G2	(416) 362-6092
Cdn. Life & Health Insurance Assoc.	1 Queen St. E., #1700	Toronto	ON	M5C 2X9	(416) 777-2221
Cdn. Life & Health Insurance Assoc.	1001 Boul. De Maisonneuve, #630	Montréal	QC	H3A 3C8	(514) 845-6173
Cdn. Institute of Financial Planning	151 Yonge St., 5th Floor	Toronto	ON	M5C 2W7	(416) 865-1237
Canadian Investor Protection Fund	Royal Bank Plaza, S. Tower, #2400	Toronto	ON	M5J 2J4	(416) 866-8366
Canadian Securities Institute	121 King St. W., #1550	Toronto	ON	M5H 3T9	(416) 364-9130
Canadian Shareowners Association	2 Carlton St. #1317	Toronto	ON	M5B 1J3	(416) 595-9600
Comp. Corp.	1 Queen St. E., Ste. 1600	Toronto	ON	M5C 2X9	(416) 359-2001
Financial Plannners Standards Council of Canada.	439 University Ave. Ste. 1710	Toronto	ON	M5G 1Y8	(416) 593-8587
Independent Life Ins. Brokers of Cda.	2175 Sheppard Ave. E., #110	Willowdale	ON	M2J 1W8	(416) 491-9747
Insurance Brokers Association	181 University Ave., Ste. 1902	Toronto	ON	M5H 3M7	(416) 367-1831
Insurance Bureau of Canada	181 University Ave., 13th Floor	Toronto	ON	M5H 3M7	(416) 362-2031
Investment Counsel Assoc. of Ont.	61 Shaw St.	Toronto	ON	M6J 2W3	(416) 504-1118
Investment Dealers Assoc. of Cda.	121 King St. W., #1600	Toronto	ON	M5H 3T9	(416) 364-6133
Investment Funds Institute of Cda.	151 Yonge St., 5th Floor	Toronto	ON	M5C 2W7	(416) 363-2158
Investors Association of Canada	26 Soho St., Ste. 380	Toronto	ON	M5T 1Z7	(416) 340-1723
Trust Companies Assoc. of Canada	1 Adelaide St. E.	Toronto	ON	M5H 2R3	(416) 866-8842
Trust Companies Association of Cda.	50 O'Connor	Ottawa	ON	K1A 0S6	(613) 563-3205

Government Agencies/Related Organizations

Alberta Securities Commission	10025 Jasper Ave., 19th	Edmonton	AB	T5J 3Z5	(403) 427-5201
B.C. Securities Commission	1100-865 Hornby St.	Vancouver	BC	V6Z 2H4	(604) 660-4800
Bank of Canada	234 rue Wellington St.	Ottawa	ON	K1A 0G9	1-800-303-1282
Business Development Bank of Cda.	5 Place Ville Marie, #400	Montréal	QC	H3B 5E7	1-888-463-6232
Canadian Deposit Insurance Corp.	50 O'Connor St., 17th Floor	Ottawa	ON	K1P 5W5	(613) 996-2081
Canada Mortgage & Housing Corp.	700 Montreal Road	Ottawa	ON	K1A 0P7	(613) 748-2000
Deposit Insurance Corp. of Ontario	4711 Yonge St., #700	North York	ON	M2N 6K8	(416) 325-9444
Manitoba Securities Commission	#1128-1130, 405 Broadway Ave.	Winnipeg	MB	R3C 3L6	(204) 945-2550
Nova Scotia Securities Commission	1690 Hollis St., 2nd	Halifax	NS	B3J 3J9	(902) 424-7768
Ontario Securities Commission	20 Queen St. W., Suite 1800	Toronto	ON	M5H 3S8	(416) 597-0681
Québec Securities Commission	800 Victoria Sq., 17th, 246 Tour de la Bourse	Montréal	QC	H4Z 1G3	(514) 873-5326
Revenue Canada, Taxation	875 Heron Road	Ottawa	ON	K1A 0L8	(613) 954-2369
Saskatchewan Securities Commission	1920 Broad St., #800	Regina	SK	S4P 3V7	(306) 787-5645

Stock Exchanges

Stock exchanges often publish information brochures that are of interest to investors. Here is a list of stock exchanges.

Alberta Stock Exchange	300-5th Ave. S.W., 10th	Calgary	AB	T2P 3C4	(403) 974-7400
American Stock Exchange	86 Trinity Place	New York	NY	10006	(212) 306-1000
Chicago Board of Options Exchange	400 S. LaSalle St.	Chicago	IL	60605	1-800-678-4667
Montréal Exchange	Stock Exch. Twr, 800 Victoria Sq., CP 61	Montréal	QC	H4Z 1A9	1-800-361-5353
Toronto Stock Exchange	The Exchange Tower, 2 First Cdn. Pl.	Toronto	ON	M5X 1J2	(416) 947-4700
NASDAQ	1735 K St.	Washington	DC	20006	(202) 496-2500
New York Stock Exchange	11 Wall St.	New York	NY	10005	(212) 656-3000
Vancouver Stock Exchange	609 Granville St., Box 10333	Vancouver	BC	V7Y 1H1	(604) 689-3334
Winnipeg Commodity Exchange	#500, 360 Main St.	Winnipeg	MB	R3C 3Z4	(204) 925-5000
Winnipeg Stock Exchange	620-One Lombard Place	Winnipeg	MB	R3B 0X3	(204) 987-7070

FKI

Specialists in Financial and Pre-retirement Education

Seminars — Workshops — Training

Distributors of the Andex Chart for the Canadian Investors

Topics

Financial Planning	Social Security Plans
Setting Goals	RRSPs
Designing Action Plans	Annuities, RRIFs, and LIFs
Developing a Positive Attitude	Will and Estate Planning
Handling Procrastination	Housing and Real Estate
Power of Compounding	Maximizing Use of Leisure Time
Paying Yourself First	Second Careers
Cash Management	Volunteerism
Designing Statements	Travel
Tax Planning	Wellness Issues
Asset Allocation Strategies	Relationships
Mutual Funds	Creating a Vital Retirement Lifestyle
Selecting a Financial Planner	Retiring With Financial Dignity
Employer Pension Plans	

Financial Knowledge Inc.

Mission Statement

We are committed to be a leadership company providing financial planning and pre-retirement education. We will achieve this goal through the development, design, and delivery of the highest quality adult learning systems, educational programs, and knowledge tools that provide significant value added benefits to our participants. We ensure the participants success through the provision of leadership skills, vision, and values.

Corporate Objectives

▲ To enable employers to provide low-cost, value-added programs and knowledge tools for their employees as part of their compensation/benefits program.

▲ To serve our clients first, last, and always; to broaden their knowledge base; to take control of their financial and lifestyle destinies.

▲ To cheerlead by informing, educating, and motivating all participants to stretch and reach for their true potential.

▲ To coach by teaching new skills, with hands-on instruction in seminars/workshops, and to provide the knowledge so that participants can become their own best advisors.

▲ To help participants secure their financial future by teaching the stewardship of wealth management.

Education Programs

Financial Knowledge Inc.'s education programs address the needs of employees to learn

▲ financial self-management skills & techniques
▲ career transition and lifestyle planning
▲ lifetime investment strategies
▲ pre-retirement planning

Program formats are workshop, seminar, self-study, and train-the-trainer. Instruction and materials focus on financial self-management and making lifestyle changes for a rewarding and secure future. Our workshops use active participation by employees and spouses in developing personal goals for investing, retirement, and lifestyle planning.

Customization — Made to Measure

At **Financial Knowledge Inc.** we can tailor a program to suit your needs. We offer several standard programs, however, upon request we can design to your goals. And our trainers have the maturity and financial industry experience you would expect, to deliver this sensitive subject matter to your employees.

You may already be offering financial, lifestyle, and/or pre-retirement planning programs to your employees and you may want to take a serious look at revamping an old program or you might be looking for a new pre-retirement program to enhance your benefits program. Whatever your need, we would be happy to provide a solution to fit your corporate culture. Perhaps it's time to take a new look at retirement... your employees' future well-being may depend on it.

Financial Knowledge Inc.
Corporate Seminar & Workshop Outlines

Our goals are to educate participants in the lifetime skills of financial self-management; to motivate the individual to take action to secure a rewarding future; and to provide the tools and strategies needed to achieve financial independence and a fulfilling retirement.

4-HOUR PENSION TRANSITION SEMINAR to enhance employee awareness and understanding of pension options; to focus on the employees responsibility of choosing the appropriate asset classes to fit their needs:

- risk tolerance profiles
- asset allocation strategies
- inflation (purchasing power)
- investment selection

1-DAY FINANCIAL PLANNING WORKSHOP to address the following type of needs:

- financial self-management skills and techniques
- investment and asset allocation strategies
- pre-retirement preparation and planning
- creating a happy, healthy, lifestyle

2-DAY FINANCIAL & LIFESTYLE PLANNING WORKSHOP in addition to the topics covered in the 1-Day Financial Planning Workshop covers many other topics such as:

- lifestyle and wellness issues
- human support systems
- attitudes towards retirement
- personal fulfillment
- utilization of time
- six powers of success

2-DAY DOWNSIZING AND EARLY LEAVE WORKSHOP covers all of the topics in the 2-Day Financial and Lifestyle Planning Workshops as well as:

- career transition, challenges, and opportunities
- surviving severance and measuring options
- cash management strategies (short term versus long term)
- income tax strategies

Downsizing & Early Retirement Workshops

Our workshops provide an integral part of staff reduction and early retirement programs for departing employees and the survivors! We address the issues of wellness and lifestyle changes in all retirement planning programs.

Career Transition programs focus on wealth management and the personal opportunities presented by change.

Surviving Severance programs are excellent for addressing cash management issues, assessing severance options, and applying income tax strategies.

Financial Self-Management & Pension Transition Workshops

We facilitate ongoing employee education programs. For example, sponsors of "money purchase" pension plans and employee directed savings and capital accumulation plans use our Financial Pursuit training to teach employees asset allocation strategies/investing skills for plan investments and personal wealth.

Unbiased Advice — Fee Based
Our programs provide unbiased generic education, with no product affiliation (investment, insurance, or retirement services). Financial education is provided by trained and experienced professionals in our workshops with optional individual counselling available. We are compensated on a fee for service basis.

Presentations are sponsored by employers for groups of employees, by professional advisors for their clients, and by professional associations for their members.

Financial Knowledge Inc.
Public Seminar Outline

Graydon Watters is pleased to announce the availability of the Financial Survival for the 21st Century Seminar based on the best-selling book by the same title. The seminar always provides a current viewpoint on the markets and where to invest your money now and stresses the following major topics:

3 Major Paradigm Shifts
- A New Paradigm for Retirement is Required
- FKI's Projections — Next 20 Years
- The Retirement Gap

6 Powers of Success
- Physical Health, Personal Control, Personal Skills, Personal Fulfillment, Precious Relationships, Pursuit of Financial Freedom
- Retirement 20st Century — Balanced Lifestyle 21st Century
- The Road to Retirement

6 Major Resources at Retirement
- Canada's Debt — NIMBY
- OAS/CPP Privileged or Entitled
- Political Games — High Human Cost

Only 2 Ways to Increase Your Real Wealth
- Rehearse Your Life Plan
- Your Financial Planning Factory
- Time (86,400 seconds)
- Investment Personality Pyramid

4 Major Reasons Financial Plans Fail
- Procrastination
- Laws of Attitude
- Train of Life

4 Phases of Every Cycle
- Interest Rates — Stock Prices
- Investment Risks Can Affect Your Cruise
- Investment Cycle
- Ibbotson & Associates — After Taxes and Inflation
- The Stock Market Has Been Going Up All of Your Life
- Where is The Market Now?
- World Investment Opportunities

Only 1 Asset Allocation Solution Matters
- Your Asset Allocation Solution

Only 2 Ways to Manage Money
- Mutual Funds (Professional Versus Self-Management)
- Financial Advisors Add Value
- Relationships Don't Rust

For more information on our corporate and public seminars and workshops please contact:

Jack Wright or Andy Billesdon
Financial Knowledge Inc.
279 Yorkland Blvd., North York, Ontario M2J 1S7
Tel: (416) 499-5466 Fax: (416) 499-7748

How to Choose
a
Financial Advisor

Perhaps the greatest gift that
you could give to someone is
a personal copy of *How to
Choose a Financial Advisor*. The
book makes a great gift
for those important people in
your life: son, daughter, niece,
nephew, friend, or business
associate. *How to Choose a
Financial Advisor* is the perfect
resource for all Canadians
from the time they begin their
working careers until they retire.

Financial Product Order Form

Quantity	Item Description	Regular Price	Net Price
_____	*How to Choose a Financial Advisor* (book)	$14.95	$ _____
_____	*Financial Survival for the 21st Century* (book)	12.95	_____
_____	*Financial Pursuit* (book)	29.95	_____
_____	RRSP Calculator (slide ruler)	5.00	_____
_____	Andex Handout Chart (16.5" x 11")	15.00	_____
_____	Six Powers of Success (Ruler)**	5.00	_____
	SPECIAL COMPLETE PACKAGE		
_____	*(one of each of the above)*	$69.95	_____
	Shipping & Handling		$7.00
	Sub Total		$ _____
	GST @ 7%		_____
	***PST @ 8% (on Six Powers of Success Ruler*		
	for Ontario Residents Only)		_____
	Total		$ _____

Please ship to

Company Name: _____

Attention: _____

Address: _____

City: _____ Province: _____ Postal Code: _____

Telephone: ( ) _____ Fax: ( ) _____

Method of Payment

I have enclosed a cheque for $ _____ *made payable to Financial Knowledge Inc.*

OR

Please debit my **Visa** or **MasterCard** in the amount $ _____

Credit Card #: _____ Expiry Date: _____

Name of Cardholder: _____

Signature of Cardholder: _____

We offer discounts for orders of 10 or more on our products. Please write, call, or fax FKI for details.

Financial Knowledge Inc.

279 Yorkland Blvd., North York, Ontario M2J 1S7   Tel: (416) 499-5466 Fax: (416) 499-7748

Notes

Notes

Notes

Notes